SU
CO

WEYBRIDGE PAST

Greetings from Weybridge, showing five views

'Greetings from Weybridge', showing five views, dated 20 August 1913. This interesting card shows various local views clockwise from top left 'On the Wey', 'Flying at Brooklands', 'The Wey Bridge', 'The River & Island', and a view of St James' Church in the centre. Weybridge at this time was a popular riverside town which provided excellent leisure opportunities for people travelling on a day trip from London or one of the nearby towns. Day trippers could make use of the river by punting, swimming of fishing in it. They could also stroll along the banks of the River Wey along the tow path and admire the rural views still to be seen in the neighbourhood before the coming of the First World War and the subsequent development of the area. The inclusion of a photograph of a Bleriot-type monoplane at Brooklands is an indication of the growing popularity of aviation and motorsport at the newly constructed Brooklands race track and aerodrome. The imposing steeple and tower of St James' Parish Church is included as it has been a recognised Weybridge landmark ever since it was opened in 1848. The Victorian Wey Bridge is also featured in this multiple view card, and has been reproduced on many cards since 1913. Elmbridge Museum collections hold many photographs, as well as paintings, of the Wey Bridge which has inspired many photographers and artists over the years.

WEYBRIDGE
PAST

Neil White

Phillimore

1999

Published by
PHILLIMORE & CO. LTD.
Shopwyke Manor Barn, Chichester, West Sussex

ISBN 1 86077 086 X

Printed and bound in Great Britain by
BIDDLES LTD.
Guildford, Surrey

Contents

List of Illustrations

Frontispiece: 'Greetings from Weybridge', 20 August 1913

Acknowledgements

All the illustrations come from one source, the archives held at Elmbridge Museum, Church Street, Weybridge. I want to thank all the staff at Elmbridge Museum for their continued patience and support while I have been writing this book, especially to Michael Rowe, Viv McKenzie, Sue Slight and Cathy Barker. Thanks are also due to Phillimore & Co. Ltd, who have been tremendously patient with me over the 18 months it has taken to research and write this book. Also, many thanks to Tony Hallas for kindly developing all the photographic prints used in this book.

Finally a very special thank-you to my wife Sheila, and my boys Jamie and Ewan.

To my family,
without whose patience
this book would not have been written

Introduction

Weybridge Past is a fascinating insight into the history of a unique village in north Surrey, which has a history dating back many thousands of years. The book is my personal record of the history of the village since prehistoric times and takes in the surrounding areas of Brooklands and St George's Hill, as their stories are closely interwoven with that of Weybridge village itself.

For thousands of years Weybridge was nothing more than a little settlement of houses located next to the Rivers Thames and Wey. As it was off the beaten track, the Portsmouth Road near Esher being the main route southwards, Weybridge was bypassed by great events and was for the most part a sleepy backwater consisting of a few hovels and houses. With a small population, the village was totally dependent on agricultural production, and there was little other industry in the locality to support a larger population. The Romans bypassed the area, preferring to take a route across the Thames at Staines rather than Weybridge or nearby Walton-on-Thames. In the medieval period the village became important because of the bridge over the River Wey, hence the origins of the name, Wey Bridge. With the establishment of an Abbey at Chertsey in A.D. 666, the village was passed through by monks and pilgrims to the abbey. A small chapel was established to allow the monks to worship *en route* to Chertsey, and wharves were established to enable the tran-shipment of timbers and agricultural produce by barge to London.

Weybridge's link with the River Thames was one of the reasons why Henry VIII took the decision to build a Royal Palace at Oatlands, located just outside Weybridge from 1537. He could travel down from London by state barge and alight at Weybridge before riding onto Oatlands Palace. The roads were virtually impossible to traverse, especially in the winter months, so the obvious route to use was the Thames. Weybridge later became embroiled in national events, and during the English Civil War Charles I and his family sheltered for a time at Oatlands. Afterward the Palace was demolished and the bricks used to line the locks of the new Wey Navigation, constructed between 1651-3.

During the 18th century the village became the home of many landed gentry and retired military men, who came to live in the area because of the refuge it offered them from London and society. Two large estates dominated the village: at one end was the Portmore estate while at the other was the Oatlands Park estate. In the late 18th century the Duke of York and his German-born wife came to live at Oatlands House. Weybridge was still predominantly a small village with some very interesting inhabitants.

However, it was the coming of the railway in 1838 that opened Weybridge up to outside influence and change. The new railway gave London businessmen the opportunity to live in the country and work in the city. The large estates were broken up and the land sold off for development. Luxury villas were constructed for the middle and upper classes who came to settle in the area with their families, supported by a growing commercial sector and armies of labourers and servants.

By the end of the 19th century the area witnessed more great change as the pressure on land increased and Weybridge village was virtually rebuilt over a period of 20 years. The older timber-framed houses and shops were pulled down, to be replaced by brick and tile buildings.

Modern local government came into existence in 1895 when the Weybridge Urban District Council was established, and village life became more regulated and controlled.

The 20th century has witnessed a speeding up of change, the like of which has never been seen before. The population expanded as life expectancy increased. The open ground around the village was heavily developed for luxury housing, and new industries and forms of employment began to replace the old. Leisure and the service economy started to take root before the First World War, with golf and tennis clubs being founded on St George's Hill, as well as more working-class forms of entertainment such as football. St George's Hill was developed by W.G. Tarrant who built mansions for the rich. For those who could afford them motor racing and aviation became popular pastimes at Brooklands, where Hugh Locke-King built a massive race track in 1907 which lasted until the outbreak of the Second World War. This led to the founding of a major aircraft industry at Brooklands by the Vickers Company and subsequently to many subsidiary industries. Heavy manufacturing left the area in 1988 when Vickers, now part of British Aerospace, was closed down and the work moved elsewhere.

The fascinating story of the Weybridge area is accompanied by photographs and paintings, and is arranged in a chronological pattern with chapters. These look in detail at some of the more notable events and characters affecting the history of Weybridge. Obviously any historical account of an area's development will by its nature have to omit some information and this book is no exception. I apologise to anyone who feels a particular subject, events, or people have been left out. This book is really an introduction to the history of Weybridge village; I hope you enjoy it and come away with a desire to know more about this fascinating area.

Neil White
Elmbridge Museum
Weybridge
July 1998

One

The First Settlers

Around 25 million years ago, the Rivers Wey and Mole deposited sands and gravels on top of a layer of clay in the Thames floodplain. Then, the River Thames was a wide-open free-flowing river, akin to the American Mississippi, which periodically flooded a wide area, leaving marsh land, channels and islands, which supported a wide variety of animals and wildlife. Later Ice Ages affected the landscape again, depositing more gravels and creating the more dramatic landscape features that we know of today, such as St George's Hill, Weybridge, Claremont near Esher, and Telegraph Hill at Hinchley Wood. After the last great Ice Age the area was covered with broad-leaved woodland, which was later cleared by the first settlers for firewood and building material. This created the open heathland of the area that is still recognisable today—Weybridge Heath, for example, as well as the heath land between Esher, Cobham, Claygate and Oxshott. The rich natural environment supports many types of wildlife, including fish such as chub and tench, and birds like swans or migrating geese. It has changed constantly over the last 25 million years, and particularly in the 10,000 years since humans settled the area.

The landscape that the first humans knew, then, was largely forested, with few open spaces, and the soil was poor—as it is today. These early arrivals hunted wild animals, and gathered produce from the land that was growing wild, such as berries and other seasonal fruits. Mammoth and reindeer were systematically hunted with tools made from stone or flints skilfully worked to form a razor-edged weapon. Flints abound in the soil of the area, and were an ideal natural resource from which to manufacture arrow heads, axes and knives, which could be used firstly to kill the hunted animals and then to strip off the valuable skins and meat. Tools were also made out of wood and antlers.

By the end of the Ice Age the primitive peoples had settled beside the lakes and pools left by the meltwater. They lived in tents made of animal skins, although some buildings may have been constructed of wood. The climate of dry summers and wet winters began around 8500 B.C. and produced light vegetation with birch the main type of tree. By 6400 B.C. Britain was separated from the continent by the English Channel. The Mesolithic tools of this era have very different characteristics from the ones

1 Watercolour of St George's Hill, painted by an unknown artist on 18 September 1865.

produced in the Palaeolithic period: they have a sharper edge, called a 'trance'. Light, tiny worked flints, called microliths, were also produced. Fish were a main source of food along with duck, geese, cranes and many other species of bird. Nuts and vegetables also contributed to the diet. Dugout canoes were made from tree trunks for use on the River Thames and its tributaries, the Wey and Mole.

During the Neolithic period there was a change from hunter-gatherer societies to an arable-based farming society, when people learnt how to grow cereals such as wheat, barley and flax. Hunting and fishing continued, but the diet was supplemented by peas, beans and crab-apples. As life became more settled, specialised craftsmen and traders appeared. Corn was also first ground in this period. Around 2000 B.C. Britain was inhabited by the Beaker people—so called because their pottery resembled flat-bottomed vessels. They were also skilled in the use of copper.

The Bronze Age (2000-700 B.C.) saw great improvements in agricultural production. Settlements usually consisted of a dozen or so round

2 Photograph of the Bronze-Age bucket, found during the building of the Brooklands racetrack in 1907.

thatched huts surrounded by small fields. Spinning was practised and the people became proficient in manufacturing bronze weapons—daggers, knives and tanged spearheads. Bronze sheet was produced which could be riveted. Bronze-Age dead were buried in wooden coffins in mounds called barrows. Later, the dead were cremated and the bones buried in cinerary urns.

From 900 B.C. the Celtic tribes migrated to Britain from the continent, bringing with them iron technology which was far superior to the earlier culture. However, in other respects their life was not too dissimilar from that of the Bronze-Age peoples. Later on, there was another influx of people from the continent, the Belgae, whose culture dominated the south of England. The neighbouring tribes were the Atrebates and the Cantiaci.

There is a wonderful description of this period in the lecture notes of Dr. Eric Gardner, the first Hon. Curator of Weybridge Museum, from the early part of this century. He wrote,

Picture the neighbourhood from about 600 B.C. The Thames with its tributaries (the Wey and the Mole) running through marshes—wetter than now, but not so liable to high floods: a certain amount of open meadowland and forest, and rising out of all this the dry, treeless, open heathland of St George's Hill. About 600 B.C. England was becoming populated by people drifting over the Channel in their canoes from the continent, more or less at the mercy of tidal currents. Some paddled up the Thames and explored the tributaries. There they settled in villages, placing them where there was good grazing and the land could be cultivated. Remains of several of these undefended villages have been excavated in this district. One was on Leigh Hill, Cobham; another on the banks of the Wey, close to Byfleet Church. During the construction of Brooklands Motor Track, one was found in the centre of the ground; yet another was in the vicinity of the St George's Hill tennis courts. As time passed, the villagers found that they must defend themselves, probably against other explorers coming up the rivers, but, as the villages were built for grazing and agriculture, with no attempt at defence, this was not possible: so they did what was done elsewhere in England

and by semi-barbaric tribes today. They chose a central site that could be defended, and made their principal village on its apex—in this case on the top of St George's Hill. We call it the St George's Hill Camp.

Unfortunately, we know very little about human activity on this site, apart from the suppositions of local historians who have studied it, as there have been no major archaeological finds to give concrete evidence for the use of the hill. In his *History of Surrey* (published 1841), Brayley described St George's Hill:

> On the south-east angle of this eminence is an ancient ENCAMPMENT of considerable size, which, within the last eighty or one hundred years, appears to have acquired the name of Caesar's Camp; yet on what authority is questionable. It exhibits nothing of the regularity of a Roman work; and although, from different circumstances, it may be fairly assumed that is was occupied by the Romans, we must hesitate in ascribing its origins to that people ... the extreme irregularity of its form and outline seems strongly to militate against the idea of its being of Roman origin. We should rather assume that it was originally British, and constituted one of those hill fortresses from which our rude ancestors were driven by the superior discipline and weapons of the Roman soldiers.

In 1911 Dr. Eric Gardner published a report entitled 'The British Stronghold of St George's Hill, Weybridge', in which he described the site in great detail. At that time it was owned by Mr. Egerton, who allowed Dr. Gardner and the Rev. E.A. Downman to make a few sections on the site before it was purchased by the property developer, W.G. Tarrant. Tarrant later developed the site by building high-class residential property on St George's Hill, thereby making future archaeological excavations virtually impossible. Gardner thought that there was a main entrance to the camp from the south-west side, in a gully between Spence's Thrift and Raven's Camp. Although there have been no finds on the site it is clear that the camp probably dates back to the Bronze Age, judging from artefacts found in the immediate vicinity. Gardner pointed out that St George's Hill is surrounded on three sides by

rivers, Thames, Mole and Wey. Local finds have included Bronze-Age burial urns, or cinerary urns, which were found at St Mary's Road, Oatlands, and between St Mary's Road and Oatlands Church. These urns were made to contain the remains of Bronze-Age cremations. The pots were of unbaked clay and made by hand, not by using a potter's wheel. Other finds in the area have come from Silvermere, Leigh Hill near Cobham, and the Wey Ford, Weybridge. A number of Bronze-Age weapons, including a rapier, socketed axe heads, a palstave, a spear head, a knife and other implements were dredged out of the Wey in the reach near the Wey Bridge in 1912. These are now in the possession of Elmbridge Museum.

Dr. Gardner ended his tract by saying:

> It remains to be seen whether the developer of modern estates will have more respect for ancient earthworks ... or whether he will destroy one of the most important prehistoric monuments now remaining in the County of Surrey; for at the time of writing St George's Hill, with its nine hundred acres of woodland, is passing into the builder's hands, and the fate of the old British Stronghold is not yet decided.

In 1981 the Surrey County Archaeological Unit (SCAU) excavated the Iron-Age fort at St George's Hill and discovered nothing new to add to the work done 70 years earlier by Dr. Gardner. In 1995 the Secretary of State scheduled St George's Hill as an ancient monument.

Another interesting find from prehistory in the vicinity of Weybridge was the discovery of a Bronze-Age bucket on the construction site of the Brooklands motor-track in April 1907 on the estate owned by Hugh Locke King. This bucket was made of adjoining plate and was found while workmen were sinking a 14 ft shaft for a bridge pier in a bed of sand and clay. The bucket originated from Northern Italy where it was made about 500 B.C. for export. It was quite small, measuring 7.1 inches in height with a diameter of 7.9 inches. It had a pair of arched handles on a corrugated bronze body which had been repeatedly hammered and forged. Similar types of bucket were found in Austria, Belgium and Germany, all of which originated from Italy. The bucket was presented to the British Museum by Mr. William Dale, F.S.A. in 1907.

Brayley's *History of Surrey* mentions the Silvermere urn, discovered during the building of a house on the Silvermere estate for Henry G. Atkinson. In 1838, workmen laying foundations for the house dug through three ancient barrows and in the process found a Bronze-Age urn. It is made of unbaked clay and dates from about 1,000 B.C. It has some decoration on the heavy overhang rim. It was found with two other urns and human remains, nothing of which is known today.

The nearest centre of Roman life to Weybridge was Staines, known to the Romans as *Pontes*, a market town as well as a military outpost guarding the roads leading from London to the west country. There are few Roman remains in the vicinity of Weybridge other than a Romano-British villa site that was excavated at nearby Chatley Farm, Cobham in 1942. Some scattered finds have been discovered elsewhere in the neighbourhood, particularly in Oatlands Drive, Weybridge, and a horde of coins was unearthed at Brooklands during the construction of the motor-racing circuit in 1906/7. More coins were found during the construction of houses on St George's Hill and date from A.D. 200-300.

Many of the wealthier British chiefs adopted a Roman lifestyle during this period and took on aspects of domestic Roman living. The occupation probably had very little effect on the lives of ordinary Britons in the Weybridge area, although the rivers Thames, Wey and Mole, would have been used to transport goods, and Romans would have travelled on the many trackways through the woodland of the area.

The Romano-British villa site at Chatley Farm lies on the east of Ockham Common, between the sands of the common and the alluvial meadows of the River Mole. The countryside here is covered with heather, birch, pine and chestnut. In June 1942 Mr. R.M. Brachi saw traces of a Roman building on the river bank and the site was excavated, with the farmer's permission, by Sheppard Frere, M.A., F.S.A. The building was actually a later Roman bath-house, which would have adjoined a villa, although the river had washed this away. Four rooms were discovered: a cold bath, a warm room, a hot room and a small compartment used as a sweating room. The archaeologists noticed that the site had been adapted for use during its short history, the hypocaust chamber in particular having been later reconditioned with a flue. This bath-house was built in the period of a decaying civilisation, when the local Britons attempted to maintain the traditional amenities of civilised life. The site revealed pottery that was made locally as well as mosaic floor sections and flue tiles. Coins found on the site dated it to A.D. 320-60, after which it ceased to be used. The building may have been sacked by the invading hordes of barbarians (Jutes, Angles and Saxons), or the owners had fled, leaving it to fall into decay. Objects from the excavation are now on display in Elmbridge Museum.

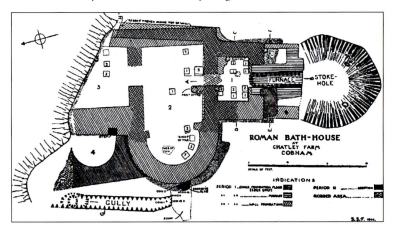

3 Ground plan of the late Roman bath-house found at Chatley Farm, Cobham, in 1942. Reproduced from the *Surrey Archaeological Collections*, Vol. XI, 1944.

Two

Anglo-Saxon and Norman Weybridge

The earliest written records of present-day Weybridge date from the seventh century when the town was referred to, in a document of A.D. 675, as *Waigebrugge*—or 'Bridge over the river Wey'. This was written shortly after the introduction of Christianity to the area by the monks who occupied nearby Chertsey Abbey, which was founded in A.D. 666 by St Erkenwald. In fact Chertsey Abbey was a Benedictine Abbey dedicated to the apostle St Peter. In time it owned much of the land in the immediate vicinity, including Weybridge, Esher and Cobham, and was one of the most powerful religious houses in early Christian Surrey. In the medieval period it was famed for its splendid decorated floor tiles. This building must have had a great psychological impact on the previously heathen Anglo-Saxons, who tended to live in very rudimentary wooden dwellings.

By A.D. 400 the legions of the Roman army were being withdrawn from Britain to protect the borders of the Empire in Italy. This left Britain wide open to attack from the Jutes, the Angles and the Saxons. The Dark Ages descended upon the land, ending 400 years of Roman civilisation and administration in Britain. The local Britons who had adopted the Roman way of life were either killed by the invaders, or fled the area. Very few of them were assimilated into the new order of things. We tend to view these tribal peoples as very backward and uncivilised, probably owing to the fact that very little remains of their culture and way of life. Most of the buildings left from the Roman period fell into disuse and collapsed or were raided for building material. The local Anglo-Saxons used the material from the natural environment and built themselves wooden houses with thatched roofs on existing settlements. They survived on a subsistence agricultural system, which depended heavily on meat acquired from hunting and fishing, which was plentiful in the area, to supplement their often meagre diet.

In A.D. 871 a fleet of over ninety Danish longships, led by the pagan King Olaf, sailed up the Thames, raiding the various towns and villages along their route and leaving devastation in their wake. The longships proceeded to Chertsey Abbey, which they systematically destroyed, killing all of the monks. The Danes were eventually defeated in a battle at Ashdown near Newbury, but the destruction of the Abbey, which was the flower of early Anglo-Saxon Christianity in Surrey, was so complete that it was not until A.D. 964 that the Abbey was reinstated. Much later, after more bitter fighting with the Vikings and the Danes, Alfred the Great of Wessex restored peace to the area. At this time Weybridge did not have a church of its own, although a church has existed in nearby Stoke D'Abernon since A.D. 700.

Little survives from the Anglo-Saxon period, although Elmbridge Museum has a Danish battle-axe that was found in a ford near the Wey Bridge and has been dated to about the ninth century and could have been used by those Danes who sacked Chertsey Abbey in A.D. 871. Other items found locally include an Anglo-Saxon iron spear head, found in the River Wey. Little other material evidence remains, the organic materials used in everyday Anglo-Saxon society, such as cloth, leather and wood, having rotted away. Other than the metal objects, few burial sites from the period have been found in this part of north Surrey.

By the 10th century Weybridge was situated in what was called the Elmbridge Hundred, one of 14 Anglo-Saxon administrative districts that covered the whole of the present-day county of Surrey. The neighbouring hundreds were Godley, Kingston and Brixton. The Elmbridge Hundred ran along the River Thames from Weybridge to East Molesey and along the course of the River Mole from the Thames to Stoke D'Abernon. This incorporated most of the towns and villages of the present-day Elmbridge Borough Council, although Thames and Long Ditton were situated in the Kingston Hundred. These districts provided the first fledgling parliaments, known as Hundred Moots, where men from the local villages were able to meet to discuss the business of their communities. The name Elmbridge is derived from 'Amelebridge', meaning bridge over the River Mole or Amele, or in Old English, Emlyn or Emley Bridge.

Before the Norman Conquest Weybridge was in the possession of Chertsey, one of the greatest abbeys in the south of England. Frithwald of Surrey gave Weybridge as a gift to Chertsey Abbey in A.D. 673 and in A.D. 933 this gift was confirmed by King Athelstan. The Anglo-Saxon kingdom was rudely shaken when the Norman King William landed at Hastings in 1066 and beat the army of King Harold at the Battle of Hastings. This event sent shock waves throughout the villages of England and changed forever the lives of ordinary folk and their lords.

The feudal system imposed by the Normans divided the whole of the country into manors, which were held by lords of the manor on behalf of the king. It was the king who actually owned the individual manors, and thereby all the land in the kingdom, as his personal property. Also known as fiefs, or fiefdoms, these manors were held by the lords on condition that they provided the king with his homage and tribute. Only two

4 St Mary's Church, Stoke D'Abernon, photographed on 1 May 1906.

Anglo-Saxon magnates remained in possession of their lands; the rest were stripped of their property, which was given by William to his fellow Norman knights as a reward for their help in defeating King Harold. Lords of the manor could be laymen, such as knights, especially those William had brought with him; churchmen, such as bishops; or ecclesiastical bodies, such as abbeys and monasteries. Richard of Tonbridge was in possession of the fiefs of Stoke D'Abernon, Walton-on-Thames and the manorial lands at Apps Court in the Elmbridge Hundred and East Molesey and Long Ditton in the Kingston Hundred. The Abbey of Chertsey owned land in Cobham, Esher and Weybridge, while another religious house, the Abbey of the Holy Cross of St Leufroy, held lands in Esher of the original manor.

The Domesday Survey of 1086 was commissioned by William the Conqueror who ordered his officials to carry out an audit of all his possessions in the country. This gives us a vivid and unique glimpse into the nature of Weybridge at the time. The entries for Weybridge read as follows:

> Herfid holds WEYBRIDGE from the Bishop. Two sisters held it before 1066; they could turn where they would with their land. Then it answered for 4 hides, now for 2 hides. 1 villager and 1 smallholder. Meadow, 16 acres; woodland at 5 pigs. The value is and was 40s. When the Bishop took possession of this land, they did not have a deliverer or the King's writ for it; so the Hundred testifies.
>
> In WEYBRIDGE the Abbey [Chertsey Abbey] has hitherto held 2 hides itself. Alfred held them before 1066 and later. He could turn wherever he would. Then and now 2 hides. 3 villagers. Meadow, 8 acres; woodland, 2 pigs. (Value) always 20s.
>
> In the same village an Englishman has 2 hides from the Abbey itself. He held them himself before 1066 and could turn with the (land) where he would. 1 plough there. 2 villagers with ½ plough. Meadow, 8 acres; woodland 2 pigs. The value is and was 20s.

It is interesting to note that in the original 1086 manuscript Weybridge is referred to as 'Webruge'.

At the time of the Domesday Survey the population of the whole of the Elmbridge Hundred area was very small indeed, probably no more than 133 villagers, who held strips of land, 11 smallholders, and 47 cottagers, who held no land at all but worked full time for the richer landowners. There were also 25 serfs, who were the lowest class of all in the Norman feudal system (effectively slaves). All in all there were probably no more than 1,000 people living in the whole district in 1086, in an area covering over 20,000 acres, which consisted of large expanses of wild heath land and woodland. Only three churches are mentioned in the Elmbridge Hundred: at Stoke D'Abernon (which is probably the oldest church in Surrey), West Molesey and Walton-on-Thames. There was no church building in Weybridge nor any religious houses in the vicinity, except at Sandown outside Esher village and, of course, nearby Chertsey Abbey. The Bishop mentioned in the text is Bishop Odo of Bayeux who came over with William the Conqueror in 1066 and fought at the Battle of Hastings. It was he who rallied the Norman knights at Hastings when they thought William had died in the fighting. Bishop Odo was Abbot of Chertsey in A.D. 1084, two years before the Domesday Survey was commissioned.

Three

Middle Ages and Tudors

Little is heard of Weybridge in official records until the 13th century when, in a document dating from 1284, during the reign of King Edward I (1272-1307), the village is recorded as 'Waybrugg'. In his *History of Surrey* Brayley also notes that Weybridge was held 'in free socage of the abbey of Chertsey by Godfrey de Lucy. The estate contained in demesne twenty acres of arable land.'

At this time Weybridge was little more than a hamlet nestling beside the River Wey. A simple wooden bridge provided access for the monks and pilgrims travelling to Chertsey Abbey. The hamlet would have comprised a few wooden huts and shelters situated along the present-day High Street and Church Street. Most of the dwellings were single-storey wooden lath and plaster buildings with thatched roofs and unglazed windows protected by wooden shutters. Glazing was a luxury available only to the very rich and the church. All buildings relied on local materials for their construction: wood cut from the forest, mud and reeds from the rivers and marshes for lath and plaster walls, and thatched roofs. Families would sleep, eat and socialise together in the same room.

Local people all had a smallholding on which they would grow their own vegetables and graze their chickens, pigs and goats. Drinking water was collected from the River Wey. Sewage was deposited into cesspits which were dug in the vicinity of the dwellings, providing a rude form of toilet. Disease was rife and life expectancy for peasants was very short; those who lived beyond the age of thirty years were considered old. It was even shorter during the periodic outbreaks of plague and infectious diseases—the worst of which

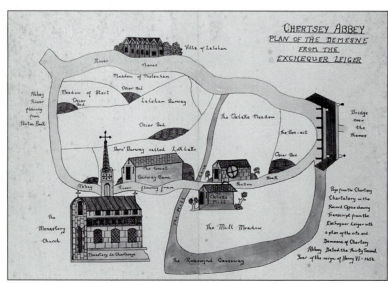

5 Plan of the demesne of Chertsey Abbey from the Exchequer Leiger. Copied from the original by Frank Carey, 1953.

was the Black Death of 1348 which swept away a third of the population of Europe, and decimated small rural hamlets such as Weybridge. At Esher the Priory of Sandown (the site now occupied by Sandown Park Race Course) was nearly wiped out by the plague.

For the better off, living conditions were not that much better, although they lived on a grander scale. The dwellings they occupied were great open halls very similar to those built by the Anglo-Saxons. A typical example was discovered at Brooklands, and dated to the period 1175-1300. It consisted of a lightly framed wooden building supported on wooden foundation posts sunk into the ground. The site consisted of several buildings, including a separate kitchen block. The main house contained rooms in line with each other, such as a bedchamber (known as a *camera* or *thalamus*) and heated rooms (*domus privata*). Very few of the houses built in Surrey in the early Middle Ages survive today, and none in the Weybridge area. The earliest surviving example in the immediate vicinity is the Manor House at Walton-on-Thames. This is a typical manor house of the period, with a large open hall at its centre, with ground and first-floor rooms at either end of the house. This property was the manor house of Walton Leigh until the estate was purchased by the Crown in 1537. After the enclosure of the 1800s the surrounding land was sold off to local farmers, leaving the house, which was rented out to tenants. It was eventually rescued from dereliction in the early 1900s by Mr. Lowther Bridger, who restored it. It remains in private hands and is now a fine example of the type of building that would have been common in the area six hundred years ago. The house is sometimes opened up for viewing by the public.

There may have been a small church or chapel in Weybridge in the late Anglo-Saxon period although none was mentioned in Domesday Book. There is reference to a chapel in Weybridge in Alexander III's Papal Bull of 1176, which confirms that manors in the area were held by the Abbey of Chertsey. By 1200 the Abbey had sold the advowson of the Weybridge church to Newark Priory, near Ripley (an advowson being the right of presentation to

6 & 7 Exterior and interior views of the Manor House at Walton-on-Thames, 1980.

the living of the church). By 1262 Newark Priory obtained a licence for the appropriation of the Weybridge church which allowed it to appoint a priest, hold church property and collect tithes (or 10 per cent of income) from the local populace. Once the tithes were collected a percentage of the income was used for the employment of the parish priest. By 1450 the first rector was appointed by John Penycoke.

The church has had a rector ever since, rather than an incumbent vicar.

The economy of the village depended mainly on arable farming, the rearing and grazing of animals on the meadow lands adjacent to the local rivers, and the loading and unloading of goods at the Weybridge wharves. Raw material, especially timber felled in the great forests in the interior of Surrey, was brought to Weybridge by road for transportation to London by barge. There is some evidence to suggest that the timber used for the construction of the Great Westminster Hall at the Houses of Parliament was transported from the Weybridge wharves.

In the Middle Ages the population of Weybridge was no more than a few hundred souls. Dr. Eric Gardner wrote in 1910:

> Some insight into village life in Weybridge may be gathered from a document of 1340, which sets forth very distinctly the duties of the tenants of the manor with regard to the harvesting of the crops of their feudal lords. Fifteen tenants had to plough at the Lent sowing for one day, receiving from the lord one meal, that is every two men had bread, pottage, ale, and one dish of meat or fish, and cheese, and each of them harrowed at the same season, receiving one loaf worth ½d. and two measures of oats for his horse, while 18 tenants hoed for two half days each. Eighteen tenants mowed all the meadows of Weybridge, carried the hay and put it into cocks, and received nine pence a day each and their mid-day meal; and when the great meadow was mown, the lord, conforming to a certain custom called mede ale, gave them each one bushel of rye, one sheep or 12 pence, one cheese value 4d., flour, oats, and salt worth 1d., and brushwood for cooking their food. When the harvest was cut 15 tenants were deputed to provide cartage and take it to the Weybridge Quay, or the Byfleet Weir, and two men had to be found to make it into cocks after it had been carted. The carting took two whole days, and two meals a day were provided. Equally minute directions are laid down for the harvesting of the rye and corn.

This pattern of life was to change with the coming of the Tudor monarchy, and in particular the reign of King Henry VIII was to have a great and lasting impact on the life of the village.

From 1537 Henry VIII started to build a royal palace on the outskirts of Weybridge at a place called Oatlands. The name derives from the first recorded owner of the land, a certain Robert atte Otlond who is mentioned in a document of 1290. The family name may have referred to land where oat crops were grown. In later records, the name is constantly changed: in 1294 it is recorded as William atte Otlonde and in 1295 as Robert de Ottelond. The early history of Oatlands is tied up with the manor of Hundlesham, which was one of the two manors in the area, the other being Weybridge.

Hundlesham Manor was originally called Huneuualdesham and it was granted to Chertsey Abbey in A.D. 673 by Frithwald of Chertsey. He also granted the Weybridge manorial lands to the Abbey at the same time. By A.D. 933 the lands was known as Whone Waldesham, and in 1086 this manor was usurped by Bishop Odo of Bayeux. By 1235 it is recorded as Hunewaldesham. In 1252-3 the land of this manor was conveyed to Sarah de Wodeham and it appears that one James de Wodeham, possibly her son, appears in possession of the property. By 1290 we hear that Robert de Oteland had conveyed land to James de Wodeham, who was the son of the James mentioned above. By 1485 a John de Wodeham had died and the manorial lands were seized by his daughter and heiress, Marjory Waker. In 1505 Sir Bartholomew Rede, a wealthy London merchant and silversmith, seized land at Oatlands. Dr. Eric Gardner writes:

> Elizabeth and William took possession not only of Oteland but also of Hundlesham Manor; Marjory Waker and her son Thomas went to law with them. The Redes claimed that there was no such Manor as Hundlesham but it was just a tenement that Joan Arnold (who was the niece of Marjory Waker) had bargained away to Sir Bartholomew Rede. The justice of the Redes' claim is doubtful, not only because they were rich and the Wakers were poor, but their allegation that there was no such Manor as Hundlesham was apparently untrue.

By 1534 William Rede had seized the 'Manor of Oteland in Weybridge' and several

8 Oatlands Palace, after Antonio van Wyngaerd.

9 Oatlands Palace, *c.*1559. From an original by Antonio van Wyngaerd in the British Museum, copied by Miss D. Grenside.

tenements, although Hundlesham Manor is not mentioned. By this date it appears to have been incorporated into the manorial lands associated with Oatlands. Five years later Henry VIII was in possession of Hampton Court Palace, after purchasing it from Cardinal Wolsey, who in return acquired land in Esher where he built himself a palace, the central section of which still stands today, known now as Wolsey's, or Wayneflete's, Tower. Henry VIII was determined to create for himself a vast hunting estate known as the 'Honor, or Chase of Hampton Court'. This would eventually stretch from Weybridge

to Coulsdon, and would contain two subsidiary palaces: Oatlands Palace outside Weybridge, and Nonsuch Palace outside Ewell. Henry required more than one palace to house his retinue of servants, courtiers and government officials.

He had wanted a palace in the vicinity of Weybridge for some time and had suggested to William Rede that he exchange Oatlands for the Manor of Tandridge. However, William died before a deal could be struck, leaving his son John, who was a minor, as his heir. Henry appointed Sir Thomas Cromwell as the boy's guardian and negotiations proceeded for the transfer of the estate to the Crown, much against the wishes of John's mother. On 29 January 1537 an Indenture was signed which transferred the estate to the King and in return the Rede family gained the former monastic lands at Tandridge. By all accounts the Rede family got the better of the exchange of properties.

Henry lost no time in ordering the rebuilding and enlarging of the Rede family home, which itself must have been quite a large house as the family were by no means poor. Work started on 23 June 1537. The building accounts survive and tell us a lot about the work that was involved. The first entry tells us that tilers were employed to

> rip and take out tyle of both sides of the hall roof, and also to new lath and tyle the same, also as well to unrip, new lath and tyle the one side of the roof over the parlour, and also to rip, lath and tyle the great barn, and also to new lath and tyle the roof over the stables.

Other records refer to named individuals employed in the King's works, such as William Whertley who was employed to work on the Queen's bed-chambers. Much of the building material came from the recently dissolved abbeys of Merton, Bisham and Chertsey, which were raided by the King's builders for all manner of materials. The tower at Chertsey Abbey was demolished and the stonework shipped to Weybridge for use in the foundation of the new palace. Richard Turner of Laleham was paid to ship the building material by the barge-load from Abingdon Abbey, while Master Bricklayer Deconson was paid for the cost of riding to Merton, Bisham, Chertsey and Abingdon Abbeys to secure the provision of stone for the new palace.

Medieval red and buff encaustic floor tiles were stripped out of Chertsey Abbey and transported up-river to Weybridge, where they were unloaded and taken by horse and cart to Oatlands. These tiles are world famous for the quality of their workmanship; they date from 1275 and were made by the Benedictine monks at Chertsey Abbey. Many survive in various museum collections, including the British Museum, Chertsey Museum and Elmbridge Museum. They

illustrate popular legends, tales and fables of the period, such as the medieval romance of Richard Coeur de Lion (Richard the Lion Heart), and the story of Tristan and Iseult.

The bricks used in the construction were of the typical Tudor shape with a rose-red coloured finish. They were all fired in locally built kilns, and the building accounts refer to bricks made by 'Master Karleton' of Walton-on-Thames, as well as 'Thomas Notryge' of Chertsey. Bricks were also made in kilns at Merstham and nearby Woking. Thousands of them were transported in barges along the River Thames, all the towns that supplied the bricks being on or near the river. The accounts also give us details of the cost of installing the gardens at the palace. John Gravett of Chertsey was paid for the carriage of two loads of apple trees, pear trees, and cherry trees from Chertsey Abbey to 'Otelands' at 6d. a load, while William Baldwyn of Dartfield, Kent, was paid for quick setting of the ditch around the park, with quick setts, crab stocks and whitethorn at 2d. the hundred.

Dr. Eric Gardner writes that Oatlands Palace

> bore a remarkable resemblance to the old part of St John's College at Cambridge, and, except that it had an additional storey, the second court of that college is almost identical with the second court of the Palace. The Palace covered an area of nearly fourteen acres, and for the most part was built round three main courts, two of which were covered with turf and the third paved with stone. The first court was entered by a somewhat insignificant door-way, and was bounded on the left by the high wall that is still standing, and on the right by a range of low out-houses. In front, facing the entrance, was a line of picturesque red-brick buildings, stretching into a second on either side of a great gateway, through which one passed into a second court smaller than the first and enclosed on all sides by buildings which probably contained some of the chief apartments of the Palace. Another gateway led into a further court, situated beyond the second, into which a long build-ing projected, which from its appearance may have been the Chapel. From the top of one of the gateways in this court rose a great tower, whose top-most storey was lighted by

windows giving views over the surrounding country in all directions, and on the parapet of which were eight metal vanes cast in the form of eight beasts. Two other small courts were built on either side of the third one, and beyond them again a line of buildings, flanked on either side by two great towers, formed the back wall of the Palace.

Around the inner courts of the palace were a myriad of smaller apartments and private rooms, which were described in a document of the period as 'faire, large and well contrived'. These consisted of separate rooms for the King and Queen, who had their own suites, private chambers, with drawing rooms, privy chambers, closets and bed chamber. These rooms were wainscoted or panelled, with tapestries hanging from the walls. The ceilings would have been plastered, and reminiscent of the rooms in Wolsey's Palace at Hampton Court. The fireplaces were probably quite simple in design with their Tudor arches, although some had very intricate panelling and carving. The palace consisted of many more ancillary rooms, including the servants' quarters, kitchens, storerooms and bakehouses, as well as stables and work rooms. In fact it was a miniature town dedicated to the well-being of the monarch. It would also have provided employment to local people all year round, for the palace required the constant attention of local builders, carpenters, plasterers, tilers, glaziers and plumbers, to keep it in good order for the reception of the royal court when it appeared.

It stood in a park of 538 acres, which was well-wooded and stocked with an ample supply of deer for hunting all year round. Sir Phillip Draycott wrote that King Henry VIII

... went to Otelands and in the Meads under Chertsey was killing staggs holden in for the purpose, one after another, all the afternoon, and they were warned by the trumpets and know thereby if there did enter any deer of price, and they not only coursed them with greyhounds, but with horse men with darts and spears—and many so slain the most princely sport that hath been seen, and many did escape over the Thames to the Forest, and on Thursday last the King slept at Byfleet.

Henry VIII continued to visit the palace after his unfortunate marriage to Anne of Cleeves. After he divorced Anne, Henry secretly married Katherine Howard at Oatlands. She spent much of her short married life at Oatlands before she was sent to the block for having led a 'licentious and voluptuous life'. Later in life, Henry rarely visited Oatlands and left it in the care of Sir Anthony Brown of Byfleet Park. The bulk of the palace had been built by the time of Henry's death in 1548. Various monarchs used the palace afterwards, including young Edward VI, who stayed there with his sister, Queen Mary, in around 1548. Queen Elizabeth I visited Oatlands many times during her reign and made the palace a resting place from the affairs of state. During her visits she was accompanied by a royal court including some of the ablest statesmen of her day, like Lord Burleigh, the Earl of Leicester, Sir Phillip Sidney, Francis Walsingham, and Sir Walter Raleigh. The Queen was a keen huntswoman and followed in the tradition of her father by hunting deer in the park. A local man, John Selwyn, was under-keeper of the Queen's deer and a story is told of how he leapt onto the back of a deer, plunged his sword into its throat, and killed it in front of the Queen.

Sir John Trevor was made keeper of the Park and Oatlands House in the first year of the reign of James I in 1603, and he was granted a sum of £900 to buy land for the King from those willing to sell their estates to the Crown. James I gave orders for the breeding of pheasants on the estate and also for the planting of new and rare trees. While visiting Oatlands Palace he was apparently cured of rheumatism by sitting with his legs inside the bodies of deer that he killed while hunting in the deer park. He also tried to combat the French monopoly on silk breeding by installing a silk-worm room at Oatlands, administered by John Bonnall.

James's queen, Anne of Denmark, made a number of alterations to the palace and was much attached to the site. The Dutch artist Van Somers painted a full-length portrait of her with the east side of the palace shown in the background. Anne led a life of royal extravagance while at the palace. She had an income of £6,000 a year,

10 Architectural drawing of 'The Greate Gate', designed by Inigo Jones for the entrance court of Oatlands Palace for King James I.

11 Detail of the Jacobean wall painting discovered in an upper room above The Riverside Chinese Restaurant in 1969. The photograph was taken prior to the removal of the painting for conservation at St Albans Museum Service.

to which the King added another £3,000, plus £20,000 to help repay her debts. Great banquets were held to welcome and entertain the many guests she had at Oatlands Palace, including the Venetian ambassadors.

Queen Anne was also a patron of the arts in Renaissance England and encouraged the work of the architect Inigo Jones. Jones became friendly with Queen Anne's brother, Christian IV of Denmark, and through him was introduced to the English Court. For nearly thirty years he worked on various projects at Oatlands Palace, including designing and building a 'greate gate', which appears in the Van Somers painting. Pieces of masonry from this gate are now in the collections at Elmbridge Museum. Ill health dogged the Queen and she died at Hampton Court Palace in 1619 just as she was planning another visit to Oatlands.

The famous Tradescants cared for and developed the gardens at Oatlands Palace. Tradescant the elder was appointed as keeper of the gardens at Oatlands by James I; he had been gardener to Lord Wotton and the Duke of Buckingham. He travelled widely, bringing back rare plants from France, the Netherlands, Russia and the near east including Algiers. On his death in 1638, John Tradescant the younger was recalled from Virginia to take up the post at a salary of £100 per annum, which was paid quarterly. John the younger died in 1662 and was buried alongside his father at Lambeth Church in London.

In 1625 King Charles I came to the throne. Charles's eighth child and third son was born in Oatlands Palace in 1640. The child was christened Henry by the Archbishop of Canterbury and was known thereafter as 'Henry of Otelands'.

Elmbridge Museum has a large section of a Jacobean wall painting dating from the reign of James I, which was discovered in 1969 above The Riverside Chinese restaurant. The painting, which was found on the walls of the upper room, was in an excellent state of preservation. By 1977, however, the condition of the painting had deteriorated because of damp and building movement, as well as cooking fumes from the restaurant. Conservation staff from St Albans Museum Service removed the painting and conserved it before it was mounted in a wooden frame and displayed in Elmbridge Museum.

Four

Civil War and Civil Strife

In 1641 Queen Henrietta was living at Oatlands with her children, after she had given birth to Prince Henry. Parliament was uneasy about the royal presence at the palace, fearing that the Queen, who was a devout Catholic, would attempt to bring the children up the same way, thereby jeopardising the Protestant religion and succession.

A full year before the tensions between Parliament and the Crown erupted in the fighting that became known as the English Civil War, the air was thick with tension and suspicion. Sir Edward Nicholas, private secretary to the King, wrote to Charles I about the fears of Parliament,

> [The House of] Commons asserted that though they did not doubt the motherly affection of Her Majesty towards the Prince, yet there were some dangerous persons at Oatlands, Jesuites [sic] and others, and therefore it was desired that the Marquis of Hertford should be enjoined to take the prince into his custody and charge, attending him in person. This resolution was delivered yesterday at Oatlands, and the Queen I hear gave a very wise and discreet answer, as I believe her own pen will speedily acquaint your Majesty.

The Queen left Oatlands and went to live at Hampton Court Palace, in an attempt to satisfy Parliament, leaving the royal children at Oatlands where she occasionally visited them. On one such occasion, Parliament, fearing she would abduct them and leave the kingdom, ordered the Commissioner of the Peace at Oatlands to wait in the park with a body of men from the local militia to avert any such departure. They were to be joined later by some Parliamentary cavalry.

However, a magistrate loyal to the Queen told her of these tricks, at which point she sent to London for help from friends who came down and patrolled the park on her behalf. Fortunately nothing untoward happened.

When civil war broke out in 1642, the Lord Lieutenant of Surrey, the Earl of Nottingham, proclaimed the county in favour of the Parliamentarians and their cause. His Deputy Lord Lieutenant was Sir Richard Onslow, who lived in Chertsey and was head of the Surrey militia. Surrey was an important county to the Parliamentarians because of its many powder mills

12 Print of King Charles I.

and cannon foundries which would prove useful in any war with the King. Despite these declarations, many of the Surrey aristocracy supported the King, and his right to reign without the interference of Parliament. In nearby Kingston upon Thames there was an arsenal of weapons and powder, invaluable to whichever side gained control of the town. In November 1642 Royalist troops hanged some Roundheads in the Kingston district. Weybridge supported the Royalist cause, which was not surprising given its connections with royalty and Oatlands Palace, as did Walton-on-Thames.

However, the Civil War barely touched the lives of the inhabitants of the town. In November 1642 a Royalist army advanced on Farnham and took the castle, aided by Prince Rupert's cavalry. Rupert quartered his cavalry at Oatlands Palace on 9 November 1642 and on the following day withdrew to safety in Egham. During this period the King stayed four nights at Oatlands Palace, while Rupert quartered in Walton-on-Thames, possibly at the Old Manor House in Manor Road. From 18 November he moved his headquarters from Oatlands to Bagshot, and thence Oxford. In the parish registers of St Mary's Church, Walton-on-Thames, there is recorded on 8 November 1642 the burial of, 'a captain among the cavaliers and his boy'. These cavaliers may have died in a skirmish with Parliamentary forces while Prince Rupert was probing the defences of London. The Royalist troops left to defend nearby Farnham Castle were defeated by Sir John Denham in late December 1642: in the fighting the castle keep was destroyed.

Military events during the next five years of warfare passed Weybridge by. Queen Henrietta Maria never visited Oatlands Palace again during the war years, because she fled the country to live in exile in Paris with her children. The youngest, Princess Henrietta, was initially left behind at Oatlands, but she was later smuggled out of the country, disguised as a beggar boy, and reunited with the family in France. The next time Prince Rupert visited the palace was on Midsummer Day 1646, by which time the war was virtually over and the King's forces defeated. On 29 June he left for Guildford and

eventually went into permanent exile. In 1647 King Charles I surrendered to the Scots, who promptly handed him over to the Parliamentarians. On 14 August Charles I was brought to Oatlands Palace as a prisoner, marched between two lines of soldiers. During his time as a prisoner at Oatlands, Charles issued two declarations under the name of Richard Rishton. He denied that he ever wanted to start a war with Parliament and that his own aim was to protect the Protestant religion, Parliament and personal liberty. He still hoped to come to terms with Parliament, but he had misread the political situation—many people were now calling for the abolition of the monarchy. Richard Rishton wrote that,

> His Majesty is in perfect health and body, and much satisfied in mind and far more pleasanter since his coming to Oatlands than formerly. He hopes to see White Hall ere long and there to consult with his two Houses of Parliament for the setting of a firm peace within His Kingdom.

Charles I was later transferred to Hampton Court Palace, from where he made an escape to Carisbrooke Castle. On the way he stayed overnight at Oatlands Palace. However, his freedom was very short-lived. Parliament, under the direction of Oliver Cromwell, had now lost all patience with the vanquished King, and put him on trial in 1648. He was inevitably found guilty of treason and warmongering, and was executed in public at Whitehall, London in January 1649. Soon afterwards Cromwell was appointed Lord Protector of the Commonwealth and ruled as such until his own death in 1658. He was briefly followed by his son, until Parliament and the army invited the exiled Charles II back to England as King.

After the execution of the King, Parliament wasted no time in ordering a comprehensive survey of all royal property in the kingdom, with the intention of selling it to raise money to pay the wages of the army. The contents of Oatlands Palace were catalogued, priced and put on view to potential buyers on 13 September 1649. They included 61 paintings, some from the Dutch, Flemish and Venetian schools, plus a large amount of elaborate furniture, bedsteads

13 Henry of Oatlands, Duke of Gloucester. Painted in 1657 by J.V. Bookorst.

14 Engraving by Gough of Oatlands Palace.

15 Plan of Oatlands Palace overlaid with a modern road plan, taken from the Oatlands Palace Preliminary Report by Alan Cook, 1968.

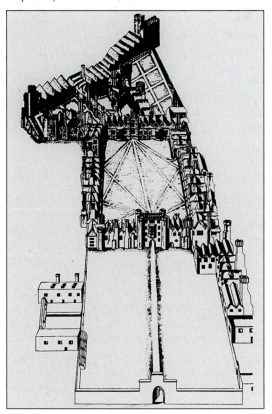

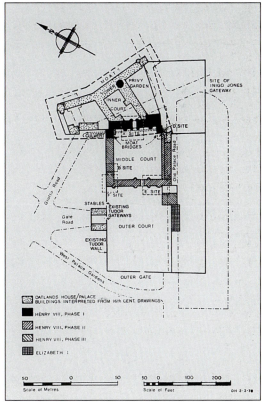

and hangings. The sale accounts testify to the items offered for sale: 'A canopie, of hair coloured silver velvet trimmed with silver spangled lace £3. Six single valences of cloth of gold, tissued and raised with crimson velvet £6. A suite of white Dymothy, containing seven pieces embroidered all over with the O's, lined with fustian £40.' The palace inventory included a listing of all the goods in the premises, including beds, chairs, and carpets from Persia and Turkey with embroidered coats of arms. Other possessions included cupboards, fire irons, tables, tapestries, screens, looking glasses, and even a brass figurine of King Charles and a billiard table. The contents were sold off and are now lost to posterity. One exception may be an ornate fireplace and wooden overmantel and surround now in The Burrell Collection, Glasgow. This was purchased by the Glasgow shipping magnate, Sir William Burrell, from the Randolph Hurst Collection and dates from the period when Henry VIII was building Oatlands Palace. The Burrell Collection also has a Tudor bedhead that may date from the marriage of Henry VIII to Anne of Cleeves. The Parliamentary inventory also records that there were five gardens within the confines of the palace site. These all had names and were called 'The Great Garden', 'The Long Garden', 'The

16   Cornice terminal from Oatlands Palace, originally from Chertsey Abbey.

King's Privy Garden', 'The Queen's Privy Garden' and 'The New Garden'.

The whole of the palace estate was put up for sale in 1650 at a material value of £4,023 18s. 0d. The sale of the palace was confirmed when 'Robert Turbridge of St Martines in ye fileds in the county of Midd. Gent., on behalf of divers originall creditors by whom he is sufficiently authorised' purchased the estate. The other creditors with Turbridge were Captain Walter Bethell, Captain Francis Bacon, Lieutenant Thomas Johnson, Cornett John Wittie, Ensign Michell Bacon and Troopers Joseph Thrushcrosse and Peter Pinder. The park was sold for £500 and 700 trees were cut down for use by the Navy with a further 400 earmarked for the same purpose. The King's prized herd of deer was sold off for just £13.

The palace itself was demolished by Turbridge and his creditors, and from 1651 the bricks were sold off to Sir Richard Weston of Sutton Place who was embarking on the canalisation of the River Wey. He used the bricks to construct the locks on the canal as well as some bridges.

Oatlands was not the only royal palace to be demolished. Nonsuch Palace at Cheam and Richmond Palace, London were both demolished to pay off Parliament's debts. Hampton Court Palace survived because the Lord Protector, Oliver Cromwell, used it as his official residence when not in London for state business. Today, nothing remains above ground of Henry VIII's Oatlands Palace, except for one Tudor gateway in Palace Gardens, Weybridge, which is now incorporated into an 18th-century brick wall.

The palace site was extensively excavated and photographed in the 20th century, firstly by Dr. Eric Gardner in the 1920s, when a council house estate was constructed on the site of the palace, and more extensively between 1968-74, by the Oatlands Palace Excavation Committee (OPEC for short) under the direction of Mr. Alan Cook, when part of the foundations was discovered amongst the gardens of the council house residents. The whole excavation archive is now in the possession of Elmbridge Museum, which displays finds from the excavation. Another

17 A photograph of the excavations at Oatlands Palace, 1968, showing the uncovered moat, bay-window and garderobe turret. The roof of the conduit is on the left.

smaller excavation was carried out in 1983-4 under the auspices of the Surrey County Archaeological Unit (SCAU).

In the immediate aftermath of the King's death, Weybridge was touched by social and political controversy when the radical Gerrard Winstanley and his followers, known as 'Diggers', occupied land on St George's Hill. Winstanley was a London cloth merchant who was bankrupted by the war. Born in Wigan in 1609, he became a freeman of the Merchant Taylors' Company of London in 1637. Three years later he married Susan King of Cobham, and in 1643 went to live in Kingston to escape his London creditors. After the Civil War the family moved to Walton-on-Thames. There he lived as a cow herder, and as a result of his poverty, experienced a vision of an 'earthly life that questioned and rejected as wholly iniquitous the hierarchical structure of contemporary English society'. He believed the time was ripe to break down the existing order, established after the Norman Conquest, which he believed had enslaved the common people in a life of servitude. Much of his inspiration came from reading the Bible.

Winstanley's followers occupied part of St George's Hill around 1 April 1649. The Council of State, a body set up to administer the kingdom after Charles's death, learnt of the goings on at St George's Hill, and reported that,

On Sunday night last there was one Everard, once of the army but was cashiered, who termeth himself a prophet, one Stewer [Star] and Coulton and two more, all living in Cobham, came to St George's Hill in Surrey and began to dig on that side of the hill next to Campe Close, and sowed the ground with parsnips, carrots and beans. On Monday following they were there again, being increased in their number, and on the next day, being Tuesday, they fired the heath and burned at least 40 rood of heath, which is a very great prejudice to the Towne. On Friday last they came again, between twenty and thirty, and wrought all day at digging. They did then intend to have two or three ploughs at work, but they had not furnished themselves with seed-corn, which they did on Saturday at Kingston. They invite all to come and help them, and promise them meat, drink and clothes. They do threaten to pull down and level all park pales, and lay open, and intend to plant there very shortly. They give out they will be four or five thousand within ten days, and threaten the neighbouring people there; that they will make them all come to the hills and work; and forewarn them suffering their cattle to come near the plantation; if they do, they will cut their legs off. It is feared they have some design in hand.

18 The Diggers' encampment on St George's Hill, *c.*1649, as depicted in Kevin Brownlow and Andrew Mollo's film, *Winstanley*, made in 1975.

The Winstanley tract entitled 'The Law of Freedom' made the case for the abolition of land ownership and the creation of a utopian society, which was inspired by biblical prophecies.

Lord Fairfax, the Lord General of the Commonwealth army, dispatched Captain Gladman to investigate the strange events in Weybridge. Winstanley and his accomplice, Everard, appeared before Lord Fairfax in Whitehall, London, to defend their actions; Fairfax was sympathetic to their cause and let them go with a warning not to disrupt the peace. In July an action for trespass was brought against the Diggers in the court at Kingston. They lost the case, and without the funds to pay for the court fees, their cattle and goods were removed by bailiffs from the encampment at Weybridge. Local people were very hostile to the Diggers and skirmishes broke out, involving troops who were bribed by the local landowners. Winstanley wrote that,

> Officers of Mr. Drake [a Lord of the Manor] came to my house and drove away 4 cows, I not knowing it. They took away my cows, which were my livelihood, and beat them with their clubs, so that their heads and sides did swell which grieved tender hearts to see.

And yet these cows never were upon George-Hill nor digged upon that ground, and yet the poor beasts must suffer because they gave milk to feed me. But strangers made rescue of these cows, and drove them out of the Bailiffs hands, so that the Bailiffs lost them.

Winstanley soon left Weybridge and set up another Digger community at Little Heath, Cobham. By 1650 the Diggers' camp at St George's Hill was destroyed and the site guarded by hired local men to keep the Diggers off. Little is known of Winstanley after 1650, except that he went to work for Lady Eleanor Davies, a self-proclaimed prophetess, at Pirton, Hertfordshire. It seems that Winstanley may also have been involved with the early Quakers in Cobham in the 1660s. No one is certain when Winstanley died; there was a Winstanley living in Cobham who died in 1676 aged 62 years of age. However, it is unclear whether this is the Winstanley of St George's Hill. The utopian experiment on St George's Hill had lasted under one year yet the legacy left by Winstanley and his followers has had a profound influence on successive generations of political thinkers and philosophers.

Five

The Great Estates

From the late 17th century Weybridge was dominated by two large and important estates located at either end of the village. They were the Oatlands Park and the Portmore Park estates.

When Charles II was restored to the throne in 1660 Oatlands Palace was no more and the great park where Henry VIII, James I and Elizabeth I had hunted deer presented a very sorry sight indeed. Nearly 1,000 trees had been felled and used for shipbuilding. Only a small lodge was left in the treeless park. The Queen Dowager, former Queen of Charles I, returned to Oatlands from exile in 1660 but, as there was no proper house left for her to live in, opted to reside instead at the Queen's House, Greenwich. The Oatlands estate was then leased to John Harvey of Ickworth, Suffolk, in 1660.

Brayley writes:

In 1661, Henry Jermyn, earl of St Albans, the favourite, and afterwards the second husband of the said Queen, had a lease of this manor granted at his nomination to John Harvey, of Ickworth in Suffolk, February 25th, 1661, for a term of forty years from the 3rd of October last past, if the Queen should so long live, at an annual rent of twenty pounds. The queen died on the 10th of August 1669; and by lease dated March 31st, 1671, King Charles the Second demised the estate to John Staley, goldsmith of London, and Martin Folkes, of Gray's Inn, who, as Manning observes, were doubtless trustees for the earl of St Albans. This lease was for thirty-one years, at the rent of twenty shillings a year; and in 1682, the earl had a grant for an additional term of eleven years from the termination of the last lease. He sold his interest in the property under these leases to

Sir Edward Herbert, who obtained from James the Second a lease of the estate in reversion, for seventy six years after the expiry of the preceeding grant.

Sir Edward Herbert was chief justice of the King's Bench, and had fled to France with the exiled King James II after the bloodless revolution of 1688, when William of Orange was offered the English throne by Parliament. Herbert only enjoyed two years at Oatlands, which, according to the diarist John Evelyn, writing in 1687, was 'a barren place'. Sir Edward Herbert died on the continent in 1698. His brother, Arthur, who had wisely backed Parliament and William of Orange, became Rear Admiral of England and Master of the Robes, and was made Earl of Torrington after commanding William's invasion fleet in 1688. However, he fell from favour after failing to beat the French in a naval engagement off Beachy Head in 1689. A third brother, Colonel Charles Herbert, petitioned for the restoration of Oatlands to the family in 1691 but was unfortunately killed at the Battle of Aughrim. (The petition was on the grounds that William of Orange had taken the lease away after Sir Edward Herbert had gone into exile with James II in 1688.)

The Earl of Torrington acquired Oatlands in 1696 as a grant in fee-simple, which was awarded to his brother-in-law, John Agar. He soon quarrelled with John and on his death in 1716 left Oatlands to Henry Pelham Clinton, 7th Earl of Lincoln. Clinton remodelled the estate and laid out new gardens in 1725, as well as erecting a house on the terrace. The house, which suffered a fire in 1794 (see p.24), was built in the fashionable Palladian architectural style. The 7th Earl died in 1728 and was succeeded by his eldest son, George, who was only 13 years old. However, he died in 1730 aged just 15. He was followed by Henry, who was the younger son. In 1744 Henry married Catherine, daughter of Henry Pelham of Esher Place, whose brother, the Duke of Newcastle-under-Lyme, had lived at Claremont. On the death of the Duke of Newcastle in 1768, the title passed to Henry, because the Duke was childless. Henry therefore became the Second Duke of Newcastle-under-Lyme and the 9th Earl of Lincoln. According to the social diarist Napier, Henry was an 'indolent hypochondriac'; he was also described by Horace Walpole as a 'political weather glass, his quicksilver either up at insolence or down at despair'.

Because of his relationship with Pelham, Henry acquired many titles, most of which were symbolic, including those of Lord-Lieutenant of Cambridgeshire, Master of the Jewel Office and High Steward of Westminster. Henry made up for his lack of political talents by commissioning beautiful gardens for Oatlands in the fashionable English style. This work led to the destruction of the formal gardens previously laid out by the 7th Earl of Lincoln. The less formal look was based on the fictional arcadian landscapes popularised by 17th-century artists such as Claude Lorrain and Poussin. William Kent, who was working at nearby Esher Place, was employed by the Earl to redesign Oatlands Park. However, he died after only one year's work. During his time at Oatlands he was responsible for the construction of the Temple of Vesta, a mock-ruined temple with pilasters of the Corinthian order supporting a high coffered dome. His other work involved recreating Inigo Jones's classical gateway, which had survived the ravages of the Commonwealth period. After Kent's death, Mr. Wright was employed to oversee the work at the park, including the building of the Broadwater lake and the planting of many trees, with advice and help from Joseph and Josiah Lane of Tisbury, who were employed to transform Wright's Grotto into a fantastic romantic idyll.

Not all the visitors were impressed by the marvels wrought at Oatlands, and Dr. Johnson thundered that Oatlands Grotto was 'a very pleasant place for Toads'. All the same, it was a very imposing structure built on two storeys, a lower level consisting of three separate rooms—a gaming room, a hall of stalactites and a bathing pool over which presided a statue of the 'Venus de Medici'—and an upper room used for taking tea and entertaining guests. The whole Grotto site was constructed between 1760-78, with most of the work done by the Lanes between 1770-8. The whole edifice was decorated with volcanic tufa, giant ammonites, brain coral and even horse teeth. Horace Walpole remarked in 1788 that 'I am to go thither to-morrow to see the Grotto,

19 A print of Oatlands Park when it was in the possession of Henry Pelham Clinton, 9th Earl of Lincoln, 1759.

20 A print of Oatlands House, the seat of the Duke of York, *c*.1810.

which I have neglected hitherto though ... much within my reach.' He was disappointed however by what he saw: 'Woe is me! I don't know whether it is time that I am grown old and cross, but I have been disappointed. Oatlands that my memory had taken into its head as the centre of Paradise, is not half so Elysian as I used to think.'

After 1788, when Newcastle left Oatlands, another more famous owner took up residence, as Brayley remarks in his *History of Surrey*:

> ... the duke of Newcastle sold to the late Frederick, duke of York, the estate of Oatlands, and the manors and lands which he held on Crown leases. The duke of York likewise purchased an estate with a house at Byfleet, which had belonged to General Cornwall; Brooklands, a home belonging to George Paine, esq., in the parish of Weybridge; and much other property, from various persons, both in this parish and in those of Byfleet and Walton.

The Duke of York had paid £33,000 for the freehold on the property in around 1790. In 1791 he married the Crown Princess of Prussia, Frederica Charlotte Ulrica Catherine. In a letter to his old friend and school tutor Grenville, the Duke wrote that, 'I have no doubt of being perfectly happy. The Princess is the best girl that has ever existed and the more I see of her, the more I like her.' Brayley mentions details of their wedding. The Duke of York married in

Berlin in 1791, and the royal couple had trouble getting back to Britain as they had to travel through revolutionary France:

> The royal pair having quitted Prussia, after passing a week at the palace of Herenhaussen, and a few days at Osnaburgh, proceeded by Brussels to Lisle. At this period the French revolution had commenced, and the name and ensigns of royalty were regarded with prejudice in that part of the continent. Hence, when the illustrious travellers reached Lisle, they were much annoyed by the lower classes of the people, and the arms and regal ornaments on their carriage were defaced, and almost obliterated. At length they reached Calais, and embarking on board a yacht provided for them, they landed safely at Dover, November the 17th, and the following day arrived in London.

However, the Duke soon tired of provincial life at Oatlands and of his German princess. He much preferred the royal court in London where he could frequent the gambling houses and smart clubs where he dined and played cards with his friends. In London he could also conduct a number of amorous liaisons away from the Duchess. From 1793 the Duke was employed on military service, seeing active duty in the Netherlands. Later on, he spent many years administering army reforms from his office at Horse Guards, London. The Duchess, on the other hand, shunned the high society life of

London and preferred instead the seclusion and isolation of rural Weybridge. She lavished her attention on a large collection of pet dogs, much to the annoyance of her guests. One of them, the diarist Wilkes, drily observed that, 'There were some twenty or thirty of different sorts in the house; and many a morning have I, to my annoyance, been awakened from an incipient slumber, after a long sitting at whist, by the noisy pack rushing along the gallery next to my bedroom, at the call of Old Dawe, the footman, to their morning meal.' During a period of twenty years the Duchess buried over sixty dogs in her pet cemetery at Oatlands, erecting little head-stones above each grave with the name of the dog. She even established a menagerie at the house. This included a Brahmin bull, Australian wallabies, rare goats, fowls and peacocks. Despite her eccentric nature, the Duchess was devoted to the life of the village and often supported local schools and charities for the public good. In their turn, the villagers adored her and all she did for them.

Oatlands House suffered a fire in June 1794 which burnt down one wing. This gave the Duke the opportunity to have the house rebuilt in the fashionable Gothic style with crenellated wings, turrets and gables—all of which seemed out of place on the original Palladian-style building. By the early 1800s the Duke only appeared at

Oatlands at the weekends to act as host at the numerous parties and social events organised by the Duchess. The fashionable London set quite often came down to Oatlands by coach, and figures such as Beau Brummel frequented the house and grounds. In 1816 the Duchess of York let her niece, Charlotte, daughter of the Prince of Wales who became George IV, stay at Oatlands after her marriage to Leopold, Duke of Saxe-Coburg Gotha. The royal couple soon left to live at their new home at Claremont, Esher, which had been purchased specially for them by Parliament. Tragedy struck the royal pair when Charlotte died in childbirth in 1817. Her husband later went on to become King of the Belgians.

In 1820 the Duchess of York died. She was so affectionately regarded by the villagers that in 1822 they erected a monument in her memory on the Bull Ring Square in Weybridge. It has been known as Monument Green ever since. The column used for the monument originated from London, where it stood at the junction of seven streets in the parish of St Giles in the Fields. It was surmounted by a six-sided stone, thereby gaining the name of Dial Stone. It had been pulled down in 1778 by a mob looking for hidden money, supposed to be buried underneath. It was never re-erected, and was later sold to a gentleman at Addlestone, where it lay in his garden at Sayes Court. In 1821 Mr.

21 The Duchess of York's Menagerie at Oatlands Park, *c*.1800-20.

22 A drawing of the Duchess of York's memorial in St Nicholas Church, *c*.1841.

23 The monument erected to the memory of the late Duchess of York in Weybridge, 1822.

Tod, a Weybridge innkeeper, bought the monument and had it erected by public subscription in memory of the Duchess of York. The inscription on the monument reads:

> This Column was erected by the inhabitants of Weybridge and its vicinity on the 6th day of August 1822 by voluntary contribution and token of their sincere esteem and regard for Her Late Royal Highness Frederica Charlotte Ulrica Catherine, Duchess of York, who resided for upwards of thirty years at Oatlands in this Parish exercising every Christian virtue and died on the 6th day of August 1820.

The Duke of York now lost all interest in living in Weybridge and in 1824 sold the estate to the Regency dandy, Edward Hughes Ball Hughes, for £145,000. Sadly, the Duke died in 1828. Ball Hughes, who was known after 1819 as Hughes Ball Hughes, lived off an inherited fortune acquired by his grandfather, Sir Edward Hughes, in naval service. Hughes was known as 'The Golden Ball' because of his reckless gambling and high living. He often went hunting on his Oatlands estate, although as he was no huntsman he took with him servants to load his gun, much to the mirth of the local people. In 1823 he had luxury villas for the business classes coming into the area after the arrival of the railway in 1838. At this point we leave Oatlands Park.

The other great estate was Portmore Park, now remembered in Portmore Park Road and Portmore Park Estate, which today consist mainly of Victorian and Edwardian villas. The beginnings of this estate date back to the 1670s, when the Duke of Norfolk purchased copyholdings of the Manor of Byfleet, of which Weybridge was a part. The Duke's first wife had died in 1662, and he then married his long-standing mistress, Jane Bickerton. The Duke employed William Talman to build him a mansion on land situated between the present-day Balfour Road and the Wey bridge at a cost of £10,000—a massive fortune in those days. However, Sir John Evelyn visited the Duke's new home and wrote in his journal that, 'I went to visit the Duke of Norfolk at this new palace in Weybridge, where he had laid out in building £10,000 on copyhold in a miserable barren sandy place by the street side; never in my life had I seen such great expense to so small purpose.'

The Duke died in 1684 leaving the house to Jane, who then married the Hon. Thomas Maxwell. The mansion house was then sold in 1688 to King James II who presented it to his mistress Catherine Sedley, who became Countess of Dorchester. The house was known thereafter as Dorchester House. James II is reputed to have spent his last night in England at Dorchester House before fleeing to France in exile in 1688. During 1689-90 Catherine met David Colyear while staying at one of her estates in Ireland. Colyear had conveniently transferred his allegiance to William and was serving with him in Ireland at the time. David Colyear married Catherine in 1694 and the couple went to live at Dorchester House, Weybridge. In 1699 William III made Colyear Earl of Portmore, and from then on the property in Weybridge was known as Portmore House. He was made 1st Earl of Portmore in 1703.

1702 was an important year in the history of Weybridge. At the time England was at war with France and Spain. Lord Portmore was a

24 Caricature of Edward Hughes Ball Hughes, known as 'The Golden Ball', 1819.

married Maria Mercandotti, a beautiful dancer, but by 1828 the marriage was in ruins. By this time he was seriously in debt and, in the manner of bankrupt English aristocrats, fled to France to escape his creditors. In his absence, Hughes agents leased the estate to Lord Egerton M.P. When his lease expired, Egerton purchased land on St George's Hill and built a new house there. The Oatlands estate was unsuccessfully offered for sale in 1843 by Hughes solicitors. A successful sale occurred in 1846 when the whole estate was divided into 64 lots. This time the lots were sold to property developers looking for land to build

Colonel in the Royal Scots Greys and took part in the Battle of Vigo Bay, fought off northern Spain. A British fleet intercepted a joint Franco-Spanish treasure fleet sheltering in Vigo Bay and attacked it. Four men involved in the action made vast fortunes in prize money and came to settle in Weybridge and nearby Walton-on-Thames. Vice-Admiral Hopson and Captain Jennings, who had both served on the leading British warships involved in the battle, eventually settled in houses in Weybridge. Two military men involved in the attack were also to live in the area. They were Lord Portmore, already living in Weybridge, and the Viscount Shannon, who was to settle at Ashley House, Walton-on-Thames. Portmore actually saw very little of Weybridge at this time, as from 1711 he was serving as Commander-in-Chief of all British forces in Portugal.

William Talman was again employed to improve the Earl's house, this time in the early 1700s. Two sons were born to Lord Portmore and Catherine: David in 1698, followed by Charles in 1700. Catherine died in 1717 and her husband in 1729. The eldest son, David, had died in 1728 so his surviving brother, Charles, became 2nd Earl of Portmore in 1728. In 1732 Charles married Juliana, the recently widowed Duchess of Leeds, who had a jointure of £3,000 per annum from her deceased husband, the late Duke of Leeds. The 1st Earl of Portmore had leased land in Hamm Court

prior to his death from the dean and canons of St George's Chapel, Windsor. The 2nd Earl of Portmore renewed the lease in 1735, and by this date the Portmore Park estate included a great mansion with adjoining gardens and fields, as well as farm land and stables.

The 2nd Earl had two daughters: Caroline, who married Nathaniel Curzon, and Juliana, who married Henry Dawkins. He also had two sons, David and William; William inherited the estate because David died young. William then took the title of Lord Milsington. On the death of the 2nd Earl in 1785, aged 85, William became the 3rd Earl of Portmore. William had married Mary Leslie in 1770 and they had six children. William's eldest son, who became Lord Milsington on his father's accession to the title of Portmore, was a gambler and bankrupt, who served some time in the famous Marshalsea Debtors Prison, London (immortalised by Charles Dickens in *Little Dorrit*). William broke all links with his wayward son and in 1802 he leased the Portmore Park estate to Colonel Mercer, who occupied it for one year.

After 1805 the mansion house stood empty and rapidly deteriorated, and by 1806 the Earl cut down and sold off all the trees on the estate in an attempt to raise some money. This period saw the rapid decline in the fortunes of the Portmore estate. The 3rd Earl was taken to court by his wayward son and charged with 'manorial

25 Front elevation of Lord Portmore's house, Portmore Park, 1810.

26 The Portmore Park pillars, 1920s.

waste' because it was said he was selling off his son's inheritance. However, little was done to make the 3rd Earl repair his properties. Manning and Bray's *History of Surrey* described the house and estate in 1809:

> The house is now uninhabited and in a very ruinous state. It stands on flat ground in a paddock bordering the River Wey, with little prospect. Near it are many very large cedars and firs, the former much broken by weight of the snow which fell in the winter of 1808-1809 and lodged on them. One of the cedars is perhaps the largest in England; at five feet from the ground it measures about 13 feet in circumference and runs up straight to a great height. It is said that it contains eight loads of timber.

The 3rd Earl of Portmore, known locally as the 'Bad Old Earl', made a will leaving the estate to his nephew James—the eldest son of his sister Juliana Dawkins. Around 1820 he purchased fields east of Mackford Lane, where he erected some ornamental pillars at an entrance gateway on the north side of the park, which were surmounted by trophies carved by John Nost, chief sculptor to the king. Their styles resembled the trophies at the gates of nearby Hampton Court. By the Victorian period these gates were in need of repair, and with the decline of the Portmore estate the pillars passed into the hands of Mr. Ward, the owner of

Clinton House. He had them preserved and offered them to the local authority. They were subsequently re-erected on each side of the new Portmore Park Road, where they still stand today. In June 1989 the ornamental stone pediment on the right-hand pillar was hit by a high-sided lorry, toppling the sculpted crown into the road, where it was broken beyond repair. After much delay a new trophy was carved and erected in 1997.

The 3rd Earl of Portmore died in 1822 and the estate passed into the hands of James Dawkins, who demolished Portmore Park House, which had stood empty for nearly twenty years. The title passed into the hands of his son, Lord Milsington, Thomas Charles Colyear. Although left out of his father's will, Thomas still considered Weybridge his home. The 4th Earl of Portmore lived in Milsington House, later renamed Minorca House, and on his death in 1835 the title became extinct as Thomas left no children. James Colyear Dawkins left the estate to his daughter, Miss Caroline Anna Colyear Dawkins, who died in 1857. The surviving relatives inherited the estate, which was eventually sold to Peter Locke King for £8,000 in 1861. The Locke King family then moved from Chertsey to Weybridge.

The break-up of these two estates in the 19th century set the scene for the widespread development of the village.

Six

Rural Weybridge

In the 18th century Weybridge was still very much an agricultural village, dominated by two very large estates, Oatlands Park and Portmore Park. However, there were many lesser estates or large houses in the area which were an important part of the life of the village.

Brooklands House

The first of these was Brooklands House situated on the Brooklands estate. The estate had been the property of Sir Bartholomew Rede, a wealthy London silversmith. The Rede family joined the Brooklands estate to their property in Oatlands, which was later sold to King Henry VIII and in turn became part of the 'Honor of Hampton Court'. The name Brooklands comes from the medieval period. In 1197 the land was known as Brokelands, or Brokeland, after Eva del Broc. In 1294 it was owned by William de la Brok. The term Brook probably refers to an area of marshy

land beside the River Wey. However, the name may also refer to the Brok or Broc family who owned the land, hence Broc-lands.

By the 17th century the land was owned by the Kidwell family and leased to the Crown, who in turn sub-leased the property to the Burchett family, followed by the Singleton family. George Payne acquired the sub-lease on Brooklands Farm in 1757 and by 1777 had built a large house and enclosed the adjoining land to form a park for his estate. On his death in 1800, the Duke of York purchased the land and incorporated it into Oatlands Park. Later, Samuel Keene had the sub-lease, followed by Edward Hughes Ball Hughes, when he acquired the Duke of York's estate at Oatlands in 1824.

In 1830 Brooklands Farm was purchased by Peter King, 7th Baron King of Ockham, who was living at nearby Woburn Park, Chertsey. The 7th Baron died in 1833 and the

27 Brooklands House in 1870.

28 Lithograph entitled, 'Garden View of the residence of OSBORN BARWELL ESQR at Weybridge, Surrey'. This property was later known as Dorney House.

family title passed to his son, the Hon. Peter Locke King M.P. The Locke King family continued to live at Woburn Park until 1861 when they built a new house on the Brooklands estate and relocated to Weybridge. The family were to have a major impact on the development of Weybridge in the late 19th and 20th centuries.

Dorney House

One of the major houses in the locality in the 18th century was Dorney House, situated at the northern end of Thames Street and probably dating back to the late 15th century. Henry VIII was reputedly educated there, and he certainly incorporated it into his 'Honor of Hampton Court' after 1538. In 1571 Elizabeth I gave her groom, John Woulde, a 21-year lease on lands in the Weybridge area including Dorney House, which had once been the property of Thomas Wynstone. Humphrey Dethick leased the premises during the reign of Charles I, and in 1650 it was surveyed by Parliament. It was recorded as having a timber hall, parlour, with drawing room, kitchen, buttery, as well as eight rooms on the first floor. It was also endowed with stabling for horses, as well as a coach house. The property had large gardens and an orchard.

The story of the house is really tied up with the story of the Oatlands estate, after the Duke of York had acquired its freehold in 1804. Thereafter he leased it to Osborn Barwell, until the Duke of York sold the Oatlands estate in 1824. In 1829 Mr. Walpole Eyre purchased it for £2,260. It was sold a number of times before it was purchased in the 1860s by William Schaw Lindsay, who bought it with other land in the immediate area, including the *Lincoln Arms Hotel*. By the 1870s the house had been considerably altered from its medieval state and Lindsay leased it out to various tenants while he continued to live at Shepperton. After his death in 1877, Lindsay's trustees continued the practice of leasing the house right up until 1936, when the whole estate was sold off for residential development.

Orchard House

Orchard House was built on land lying to the south of Weybridge High Street, off Baker Street, Springfield Lane and Monument Green. The Inwood family held it on lease from the Crown in the 1500s and owned the house until 1657, when Joshua Butler of West Molesey purchased it. Butler married Elizabeth Tenant in 1677 and made an inventory of the house. The inventory lists a great parlour, a little parlour, a dining room, two bedrooms, five chambers and a kitchen as well as a brewhouse. Joshua White acquired the house in 1697 when Elizabeth Butler died. White rebuilt the house in brick in around 1710 but died soon after. In 1711 the house was sold for £800 to Sir Thomas Hopson, who had fought at the Battle of Vigo Bay as Vice-Admiral of the British fleet. Hopson had been living in the area since at least 1700 and had been leasing Orchard House from Joshua White since 1706. Hopson died in 1717, but his wife, Dame Elizabeth, out-lived him by 23 years.

In 1745 John Duning bought the house. Duning was a retired merchant mariner, and had made his fortune by trading goods and slaves between London, the African Gold Coast and the West Indies. Manufactured goods were shipped from the Port of London to the African Gold Coast and exchanged for slaves, who were transported to the West Indies to work on the plantations there. The tea, coffee and sugar produced there was then shipped back to London to be sold at auction, and finally onto the customers of the fashionable London coffee houses. Although this was a risky trade, it did

provide Duning with the money he needed to leave the city and live in the countryside, where he set himself up in Weybridge as a landed gentleman. He lived at Orchard House until 1767 and died in 1772. His grave can still be seen in the Weybridge churchyard. Around this time, Captain (later Admiral) Clements of the Royal Navy purchased the property, which he leased out in the 1780s and 1790s. He died in Chelsea in 1797 and his son, Michael Clements, then acquired the property, and leased it in 1815 to Thomas Liberty. Liberty had the property pulled down after obtaining permission to do so in the lease, and built three cottages on the site of the house. There is some evidence to suggest, however, that part of one of the original wings of the house may have been included in a smaller house called 'Robin's Nest' located off the High Street. This property was not demolished until 1976.

Vigo House

An important house in the village in the 18th century was Vigo House, built by Admiral Hopson. The name of the house comes from the great naval victory he won in 1702. After his death in 1717 a memorial was erected in his

29 Vigo House, Church Street, prior to 1914.

honour in the old parish church of St Nicholas, listing his achievements:

> Here lyeth the body of Sir Thomas Hopson, knt, born at Lingewood in the Isle of Wight, of an ancient and worthy family there, who having served ye space of 55 years in ye Royal Navy, was deservedly preferred the rank of Vice Admiral of the Red; in which station he was ordered, 12th October 1702, to force ye boom that lay across ye harbour at Vigo, which he executed with his usual resolution and conduct, whereby he made way for ye whole confederate Fleet, under ye command of Sir George Rooke, to enter, take, and destroy all the Enemies ships of war and gallies; which was the last of 42 engagements he had been in, in some of which he received many honourable Wounds, for the service of his Country. Towards the latter end of his days he chose this place for the retreat and respose of his old age; where he died in peace, 12th October, 1717, aged 75.

The action had earned Hopson a knighthood and a pension of £500 a year. When he came back to live in Weybridge in 1702 he brought with him some ex-naval companions; he was already on friendly terms with the local gentry, including Lord Portmore and a Captain Jennings, as well as Lord Torrington of Oatlands Park. Hopson had three daughters, all of whom married military men, and two of whom lived in the village: Ann Hopson married Captain Storey,

Mary Hopson married Captain Watkins, and Elizabeth Hopson married Captain John Goodall, a Weybridge churchwarden and Overseer of the Poor. After Admiral Hopson's death in 1717 his widow moved out of Orchard House and went to live with her daughter in Vigo House.

Much later another seaman was to live at Vigo House. This was Admiral Sir Home Riggs Popham, who bought the house in 1796 but only stayed there until 1798-9. Popham was famous for developing a system of semaphore signalling for the Royal Navy which was used at the Battle of Trafalgar in 1805. The system was later adapted for land use and a chain of semaphore towers was constructed in the 1820s running from Portsmouth to the Admiralty in London, relaying messages to and from the fleet. The nearby Chatley Heath semaphore tower was part of a later system built using the technology developed by Popham.

Later on, Jegon Wellard purchased the house and lived there until his death in 1837; Wellard held the Office of Cursitor of High Court Chancery. In the 1870s the house was turned into a boarding school for girls until it was sold to the Rev. Walter Baptist Money in 1890. It remained private property until the First World War, when it became a military hospital store under the management of Dame Ethel Locke King. It was finally demolished in 1928 to make an entrance from the High Street to the new Weybridge Cottage Hospital then under construction.

30 Print showing the Battle of Vigo Bay, Spain, 12 October 1702.

Clinton House

Admiral George Clinton settled in Weybridge after a distinguished career in the Royal Navy, serving under Admiral Hopson and later Admiral Sir Charles Wager—both of whom came to live in Weybridge. Clinton was the Governor of New York from 1741-51 and was the youngest son of Francis, the 6th Earl of Clinton. George built a house for himself in 1756, appropriately called Clinton House, on land bordering the Oatlands estate and the High Street, Weybridge. He was made an Admiral of the Fleet in 1757, and when he died in 1761, aged 76, his body was taken to Westminster for burial in the family vault. Admiral Clinton's son, Henry, served in the British Army, becoming Commander-in-Chief of all British forces in America from 1778 until 1781. In 1784 Henry gave up Clinton House after quarrelling with his cousin, the 2nd Duke of Newcastle-under-Lyme. Henry had two sons, William and Henry, who both served in the British Army under the Duke of York, when he was on active service in Flanders. The youngest son, Henry, had a very distinguished military career in Flanders, Ireland and India, as well as commanding the third division at the Battle of Waterloo in 1815. Clinton House eventually became part of St Maur's Convent and School established in Weybridge after 1899.

At this time Weybridge was still only a village of no more than 6-700 people, the vast majority of them living and working in the immediate vicinity as labourers, farmers, tradesmen, blacksmiths, carpenters and merchants. As mentioned above, the small village had a large number of aristocratic families living in it. The rector of St Nicholas conducted a survey in 1724 and found that there were at least 18 families living in the village worthy of the status of gentry. There were two earls, a baronet, an admiral (many more were to follow), an army colonel and at least three naval captains and prosperous merchants. By this date the village had become a place for genteel retirement.

In this period local government barely existed, and the parishioners of St Nicholas parish church met in the vestry to discuss local affairs. The needs of the poor were the main topic of these meetings and were a major concern as the century progressed, since the vestry provided the poor relief which was a growing expense on householders in the area. Since the Poor Laws of Queen Elizabeth I, it had been the duty of the parish to provide local poor relief by levying a poor rate on all householders. Money, coal and clothing were redistributed through the vestry, and in 1725 the churchwardens purchased a cottage in the village for use by the parish poor. The acquisition of 'poor houses' continued throughout the middle part of the 18th century. In 1765 a committee was established to enquire about the various 'poor houses' that had been purchased in the village—which implies that there were quite a number in operation.

In 1766 Mr. Christianus Tealing proposed that the vestry build a workhouse for the poor as a way of centralising the services offered by the parish. Later on, in 1781, £100 left in the estate of Charles Hopton to build a village charity school was used instead to pay half the costs of building a workhouse on Weybridge Heath; this was completed in 1785. After this, the vestry stopped paying pensions to the parish poor, who were found work in the new workhouse instead. This was a radical departure from previous practice, especially the suggestion that the poor should be compelled to move into the workhouse. There was much local opposition towards the idea, which forced the vestry to amend their proposals; the parish poor were now invited to attend the workhouse only if they wished.

Most of the people on poor relief supplemented their income by keeping animals, such as a cow, on the common pasture land of the parish, as well as goats, chickens and pigs, to provide themselves with some fresh food and potential extra income. In 1790 a beadle was appointed to 'keep the Children in Awe in the Church on a Sunday during the time of divine service and to keep the hogs out of the Church yard'. Joseph Aldwin was selected, and it is recorded that after 1794 he was given a new greatcoat and hat once every three years, as well as £2 2s. 0d. a year in salary.

31 Watercolour of 'The Poor House', Weybridge Heath, 1828. There is some uncertainty as to whether this was the Weybridge 'Poor House'.

The most profound social change to affect the village life of Weybridge during this period was the Enclosure Act of 1800, passed by Parliament to enable enclosure of the common land of all the parishes in England and Wales. This presented the local landed gentry with an ideal opportunity to increase the holdings of their estates in the area. Weybridge was unusual in that it only had common pasture land and wasteland. Enclosure commissioners toured the area, dividing up the land and allotting it to its new owners. The Duke of York was able to add large tracts of St George's Hill to his already substantial holding at Oatlands Park once the awards had been granted.

The rationale for the enclosures was a simple one. Parliament had been forced to act because increased industrialisation by the end of the 18th century had led to a sharp increase in the population and agricultural production could not keep pace with the demands of the expanding populace. Common land was traditionally regarded as manorial waste—land that was unproductive. It was often used by local people

to graze their animals on and as a source of fuel. Apart from the commons, there were also common fields. These were a throwback to the feudal system, whereby individual land holders cultivated rectangular stretches of neighbouring land. When the crops grown were sold the landowners shared the money out between them. This was not a very productive use of the land and was very wasteful of labour, time and effort, not to mention crops. Disease spread rapidly from one crop to another.

The Enclosure Acts ensured there would in future be enough grown to feed the expanding urban populations in the towns and cities. However, it was often at the expense of the rural population, who became much poorer as a result. The common fields were given to new tenants and farmed as a complete field, rather than in strips.

The effects of the enclosures were to increase the holdings of the estate owners and impoverish the working-class farmers, who often left the land to find work in the new industries springing up in the towns of Georgian England.

Seven

Getting Around

Road Travel

Early man travelled on foot, following the natural contours of the land, avoiding forests and swampy land, and using dry ground that was easily crossed. Dr. Eric Gardner thought there was an old track-way running from the ancient settlement of St George's Hill down to a fording point across the River Wey which would have been shallow and firm enough for people to walk across with their livestock.

The Britons used local trackways, but did not make roads, and the Romans were the first people to create a really systematic road network for the area, to enable them to move their legions quickly, as well as their goods and produce. The main Roman roads in the south were from London to Chichester via Merton, Ewell and Dorking, and from London to Winchester via Silchester and Staines. However, there is some evidence to suggest that there were other roads, or trackways, in use in the Weybridge area at this time, because Roman soldiers and civilians must have travelled along a road from Dorking to Staines, passing Weybridge *en route*. Virtually all Roman roads at this time were made of a gravel surface packed over a cobbled base. Little physical evidence survives to prove one way or another whether there were Romanised roads in the locality of Weybridge, yet there must have been some form of road in the locality, to enable the Romano-British bath-house discovered at Chatley Heath Farm in 1942 to be built. Some of the building material used in its construction would have come from further afield.

With the decline of Rome, and the evacuation of the legions back to the continent, the excellent roads soon fell into decline. Roads of the quality and construction seen during the Roman occupation were not made again in Britain until the 18th century. The invention and widespread use of tarmacadam from the late 1800s saw a return to more passable roads.

In the 18th century, however, the condition of roads in the locality had changed little from previous centuries. The Portsmouth Road, which was the main road in the vicinity and ran from London to Portsmouth, passed Esher, Burhill and Hersham on its way south. This was the principal coaching route of southern England. Surrey had been the subject of the first Turnpike Acts: in 1696-7 an Act of Parliament was passed for 'the repairing the Highways between Ryegate and Crawley', as they had become 'very ruinous and almost impassable'. The Turnpike Trusts were formed by Parliament during the 18th and 19th centuries with responsibility for providing passable roads financed by money collected from toll-houses at strategic points along the way. The nearest toll cottage to Weybridge was at Esher, on the Portsmouth Road, near Littleworth Common. Coaches travelled through the district in the 18th and 19th centuries used the hospitality of the local coaching inns, such as *The Ship Inn*, Weybridge.

Many travellers were robbed by highway-men, whether they were pedestrians, horse riders or coach passengers. An interesting account of a local robbery is given in *The Lady's Magazine* of 1763-4:

> A few days ago, about six o'clock in the evening, as Mrs. Champain, a lady of Weybridge, with three Little Misses and her two Maids, were walking upon the Heath, under Lord Lincoln's Park pales [fences], they were attacked by a Footpad: as he appeared to be a very shabby fellow, she rather imagined him to be a beggar, and told him he was certainly in jest; however, putting her hand in her pocket, says the Lady, there is a penny for you, which he took, and then demanded the maids money, which they were very unwilling to part with, and expostulated with him for some time, till the fellow gave a whistle, and called out, Jack. This intimidated the Lady and one of her maids, who gave him what silver and halfpence they had; the other maid still refused him her money, telling him, with very rough language, she could not be robbed by such an ill-looking rascal. The fellow then walked off, and appearing to have no other weapon than a stick, the two maids threw off their capuchines, left their mistress and the children, and pursued him; and though the fellow ran with all his speed, the girls came very near him, and were close to his heels, when he took over the pales into Lord Lincoln's Park.

Travellers on the road between Chertsey and Weybridge had been routinely robbed by a highwayman, who held up coaches at gunpoint and demanded money and other valuables from the passengers. Eventually the road fell out of favour because of the number of robberies taking place. At this time there was no organised police force to capture criminals. However, the notorious highwayman was captured, and proved to be one of the Earl of Portmore's grooms, who worked at the stables at Hamm Court. The Earl of Portmore kept racehorses in the farm stables, some of which were reputed to belong to King George III. Apparently, every time this groom wished to rob a passing coach, he borrowed one of the Earl's hunters from the stables, but this was his undoing; though he was not recognised by his victims, someone did recognise the horse he was riding and he was caught and probably hanged.

In the 1790s the Duke of York, who was then living on his estate at Oatlands Park, helped purchase a coach, horses and harness for a local service that would stop at Weybridge. The total cost was £422 15s. 2d., to which the Duke contributed £300, while the Earl of Tankerville, who lived in nearby Walton-on-Thames, paid

32 Edwardian coach and horses in Church Street, 1910.

33 Moore's Garage in Baker Street, probably decorated for the Coronation of King George VI and Queen Elizabeth, 12 May 1937.

£100. In 1829 a local coach service ran between London and Chertsey, passing through the Oatlands Park estate, then leased to Lord King of Ockham. The coach passed Oatlands House around 11.30 a.m. on its outward journey to Chertsey and again at 4 p.m. in the afternoon on the return leg to London. It was run by Messrs. Thomas and George La Coste of Chertsey. In 1830 they applied for permission to continue running the coach through the park when the property was taken over by Lord Francis Leveson Gower, later to become Lord Egerton.

The introduction of the motor car in the period before the First World War changed the pattern of road transport, while the condition of the roads became much better than they had been during the days of the horse. Many of the wealthier inhabitants of the area were able to afford motor cars and cycles long before they were mass-produced, and for many families the transition from horse to motor car was fairly painless, as their coachmen simply became chauffeurs instead. Motor traffic actually became such a nuisance that many local authorities imposed speed limits in built-up areas and recorded the amount of traffic using the roads. Weybridge Urban District Council imposed a 10 m.p.h. speed limit in Baker

Street, Church Street and the High Street in 1910. In the previous year a traffic census taken on 28 June showed that 1,749 bicycles, 225 carriages, 20 motor vans, 179 motor cars and two traction engines had passed through Weybridge town centre. (The bicycle had been a cheap and popular mode of transport since the introduction of the safety bicycle in the 1890s.) Increased motor transport meant that the roads had to be resurfaced with tarmacadam, in place of the old gravel surfaces which had to be cleaned and watered in the summer months to keep the dust down. The upkeep of local roads was the responsibility of the Urban District Council, who spent large amounts of money replacing the gravel roads.

River Travel

With the large amount of timber to be found locally, it was only natural that people should decide to use water-borne craft as the chief means of moving themselves and their property. In the last one hundred years various dugout canoes have been discovered in the Rivers Thames and Wey at Wisley, Walton-on-Thames, Weybridge and Kingston upon Thames. For many years these were thought to date from the Palaeolithic and Mesolithic periods, around 20,000 B.C.;

however, this type of craft was also widely used in this area until the Middle Ages, so reliable evidence and dating of past finds is rather difficult. It is probably true to say that the finds are all post-Roman and date from the Anglo-Saxon period to the Middle Ages. Dr. Eric Gardner wrote in 1912 that:

> Major Travers, a former resident of Weybridge, reminds me that some twenty years ago a dug-out canoe was found in the roadway opposite Dorney House, at the bottom of Thames Street, Weybridge, just where the old stream of the Wey enters the Thames. In this case some pottery, roughly made and imperfectly fired, was found in it; but up to the present I have been unable to trace it. Yet another canoe of this class was found in the Thames at Kingston, and was exhibited for some time in the garden of a cottage, but all trace of it has now disappeared.

Apart from being a form of transport, boats would have been an ideal platform from which to hunt and fish.

During the period of the Roman occupation the same pattern of river use would have existed, albeit in a more organised fashion than before. With the development of London and other towns along the course of the Thames, including *Pontes* (modern-day Staines), large amounts of traffic would have been sent by barge and dugout canoe, as well as small sea-going vessels travelling up river from the Thames estuary. Narrower waterways, such as the Rivers Mole and Wey, would have only been accessible by smaller craft. Goods were shipped by the Romans to London from the Surrey hinterland, including timber felled for the London building trades, as well as agricultural produce like grain, corn, fresh vegetables, livestock, animal furs and skins, domestic craft items and pottery. Minerals, sand and gravel would also have gone up river for use in the building industry. This pattern of trade continued to the end of Roman Britain.

In the Middle Ages, the records of the Byfleet Manor refer to the 'wood hawe', or wharf, then in existence in Weybridge in the 1300s. The Weybridge wharves were probably situated upstream of present-day Jessamy Road and the Wey bridge. We know that a certain

Thomas Warner was given the right to build a wharf on land at Weybridge in 1463; he was a Londoner, and must have seen a good business opportunity in moving goods from Weybridge to London. The wharf he built was called the Crown Wharf. In 1485 Henry VII granted John Mason the office of Keeper of the Weybridge Wharf, possibly as a reward for his support during the Battle of Bosworth. From 1537, barge loads of rubble were coming to the Weybridge wharves from the recently dissolved Chertsey Abbey, for use in the foundations of Oatlands Palace. Masonry was also shipped to Weybridge from other dissolved abbeys.

However, it was the building of the Wey Navigation in the 17th century that really transformed the river traffic. The story is rather a complex one. In the early years of the century the Guildford Corporation was concerned about the loss of river trade, and a general decline in commerce. They investigated the possibility of canalising the River Wey to make it passable for heavy barges. They were fortunate in that a local Surrey landowner, Sir Richard Weston, of Sutton Place, Guildford, was interested in canals and while travelling on the continent in 1618-19 discovered the Dutch canal system with its locks. He conceived the idea of canalising the River Wey between the Thames at Weybridge and Guildford, by cuts between the great loops of the Wey, thus making a navigable waterway, with locks to control the flow of water and enable river craft to traverse difficult countryside.

In 1635 he was a member of a Royal Commission investigating the possibility; seven years later in 1642 nothing had been done to promote the scheme and, with the outbreak of the English Civil War, any work on such a project was impossible, especially as Sir Richard Weston was a Roman Catholic. After his lands had been seized by Parliament he fled abroad to Holland for the duration of the war. After the execution of Charles I in 1649, Weston petitioned Major James Pitson, the Parliamentary Commissioner for Surrey, for his help in securing his lands back from confiscation, as well as restarting the canal project. The Long

34 Triggs Lock on the Wey Navigation at Weybridge, *c.*1900.

Parliament returned his lands and an Act of Parliament was passed on 26 June 1651, in the name of the Guildford Corporation, to canalise the Wey from Guildford to Weybridge. Richard Scotcher, Major Pitson and Sir Richard Weston together funded the scheme, which cost £6,000 in all.

The scheme was beset by quarrelling between Scotcher and Pitson. Weston eventually invested £4,000 of his own money in the project, using timber from his estate at Sutton Place and buying bricks and stone for constructing the locks, bridges and lock-keepers' cottages from the demolished Oatlands Palace. Some of the higher locks were built using turf banks, although the lower ones all used bricks. Weston did not live to see the canal finished, as he died on 7 May 1652, although 10 of the 14 miles had been completed by this time. Weston's son, George, continued with the scheme which was in financial trouble at this stage because expenditure outstripped income. Another problem was that the backers of the scheme failed to pay for the land they had acquired as well as the wages of the

workmen who were digging out the river. As a result George Weston was arrested in November 1652 for his father's debts, leaving Pitson and Scotcher to finish the project.

The navigation finally opened in 1653 and was an instant financial success—over £15,000 in tolls was taken in the first full year of operation. The profits were shared amongst nine partners who had joined the scheme by this stage. Yet, notwithstanding the success of the scheme, financial arguments continued between the partners involved. George Weston's debts had still not been settled when he died in 1671, but Parliament decided to release the Weston family from them and six trustees were appointed to run the canal in their place. The canal's financial success continued. In 1664 horse-drawn barges with £4,000-worth of timber passed through the canal, not to mention other items of general cargo. Ownership changed hands several times as the shareholders sold out to larger buyers, or died. By 1723 two families had the largest share: the Langton family of Lincolnshire and the Earls of Portmore, Weybridge. By 1796 the canal was owned by the

Earl of Tankerville, owner of Mount Felix in Walton-on-Thames, and Sir Frederick Evelyn.

The traffic carried at this time was mainly corn for the various mills situated *en route*, as well as iron ore for the iron mills at Byfleet, Weybridge, Cobham and Coxes Lock, Addlestone. (Chapter 9 has a history of the Weybridge mills.) New trustees were appointed in 1828, and in 1830 William Stevens of Guildford was appointed to keep the books, bills, and also to manage the navigation for the trustees. In 1845 a lawsuit proclaimed that the beneficiaries of the navigation tolls were Charles and Thomas Langton, Elizabeth Clarke, and Caroline Anna Colyear Dawkins, daughter of James Colyear Dawkins. At this time, the Stevens family of Guildford were operating their own barges on the navigation; cargoes included corn, flour, timber, chalk, coal, bark, rags, barrel-hoops, sugar, groceries and gunpowder—a form of traffic that survived until the First World War.

Traffic continued to increase well into the 19th century, although the profit generated for the trustees and shareholders was hit by the impact of the new railway lines that were opening up the area, especially after the London and Southampton railway opened in May 1838. Both the canal and the railway existed side by side throughout the 19th and well into the 20th centuries. But it was the motorised lorry that sounded the death knell for the canal as a commercial enterprise in the period after the Second World War. Traffic was still being carried up and down the canal by the Stevens family well into the 1960s, the last barge-load of traffic on the canal being carried on 6 March 1969, but most traffic had transferred onto the roads by the late 1950s. In 1963 the canal was given to the National Trust by Mr. H.W. Stevens, the last member of the Stevens family to operate barges commercially on the Wey Navigation. Today, the canal is enjoyed by both canal barges and pleasure cruisers.

The bridge on the River Wey was first recorded in A.D. 675, when the village was called *Waigebrugge*, or *Weibrugge*. Certainly a bridge has crossed the Wey since the early Anglo-Saxon period, at a point near the original Celtic fording place. In 1571 it consisted of a wooden structure 240 ft. long and 5¼ ft. wide, which was maintained by Queen Elizabeth I, as lord of the

35 The Victorian brick and iron bridge built in 1865 to replace the earlier medieval wooden bridge. There has been a bridge here since at least the 7th century. This particular view is taken from a postcard dated 28 July 1928.

36 The Desborough Cut nearing completion, *c.*1934-5.

adjoining manorial lands. In 1808 the decaying bridge was substantially rebuilt on 13 wooden arches. By the Victorian period this was deemed inadequate and a replacement bridge of brick, iron and stone was planned using the latest techniques, which was opened to the general public on 31 July 1865. (Walton-on-Thames had also acquired a new bridge one year earlier, in 1864.) In 1939 work began on building a second bridge across the Wey, this time from Balfour Road, as a means of alleviating traffic congestion on the old bridge. Work was suspended during the Second World War, but it was finished soon after hostilities ceased in 1945.

The idea of shortening the River Thames at Weybridge was first mooted in 1816, just after the end of the Napoleonic Wars, but the scheme was ill-conceived and was subsequently dropped. Another hundred years passed before the scheme was again proposed in 1914, but work was stopped by the outbreak of the First World War. Nothing was done until the 1930s when a new channel was cut by the Thames Conservancy Board to bypass the most northerly loop of the Thames at Weybridge. The channel was officially called the Desborough Cut after it was opened by Lord Desborough, then chairman of the Thames Conservancy Board.

Railways

In 1834 a bill was presented to Parliament for the construction of a railway line from London to the port of Southampton. The proposal was initiated by a body of Southampton businessmen who wished to transport goods quickly to London from the port. The railway was to run through the Elmbridge area very near to St George's Hill, Weybridge.

The first surveyor of the new line was Mr. Francis Giles of London, and construction work started in late summer 1834. Gangs of navvies invaded the rural tranquillity of Weybridge and the surrounding towns. Many thousands of these labourers came to live in the area in wooden huts erected along the course of the line, often with their families in tow. They came mostly from the cities and towns of the north of England, Scotland, Wales and Ireland, although some local men were also employed, especially farm labourers who left the land to obtain better wages on the new railway.

The money for the venture was raised by the London and Southampton Railway Company through a share issue, for people wishing to invest capital in the project—a high-risk business as there were so few precedents at the time for making money out of a railway company. The

37 An early view of Weybridge railway station taken before the branch line to Chertsey was opened in 1848. The station is situated in a deep cutting running between Weybridge Heath and St George's Hill.

38 The *Bournemouth Belle* express train passing through Weybridge station, hauled by a rebuilt Bulleid 'Pacific', no. 35022, in May 1959. The last steam-hauled express trains ran on this line in 1967. The train is seen passing the Chertsey branch line junction and the Weybridge station goods yard.

Act of 1834 gave the railway company the powers to purchase land along the route, which had already been surveyed and approved by Parliament. Many landowners were only too willing to sell 'waste' land to the railway company for a reasonable rate, and thereby make some money out of it. A document of 1834 lists all the land purchased in every parish the railway ran through; in Weybridge, land was purchased from the estate of Edward Hughes Ball Hughes (who owned the freehold on the property at Oatlands Park, at this time leased to Lord Egerton), as well as Robert Bartropp, the Rev. H.C. Bayley and the rector of St Nicholas parish church, Weybridge, who owned a considerable amount of property in the area. Other landowners who benefited from the scheme included the Overseers and Trustees of the Poor of Weybridge, as well as the Hon. Locke King. Railway development led to a sharp rise in land prices locally; in 1834 the railway company paid £30 per acre, and by 1868 it was paying £372 an acre. A hundred years later an acre would have cost £20,000.

The building of the railway line was a mammoth task in itself. Several thousand men were labouring on the line every day of the week, using hand tools such as picks, shovels and spades to extract the thousands of tons of earth from cuttings, as well as using hundreds of thousands of bricks to build the bridges and viaducts required to take the railway over existing features such as roads, rivers, and streams, as well as the tunnels to take it through natural obstacles such as hills. These workers often lived on or near the construction sites, and would have satisfied their thirst in one of the many hostelries then in existence in Weybridge and Oatlands, or ventured further afield into Hersham or Walton-on-Thames. By 1837 over ten miles of railway line had been constructed, including a 45ft. cutting through St George's Hill. The line from London (Nine Elms) through to Woking was completed and opened on 19 May 1838, with the final section from Woking to Southampton opening in 1840. After 1840 the London and Southampton Railway Company became the London and South Western Railway Company.

Weybridge station was opened on 21 May 1838. The railway company were then charging 2s. 6d. for a single second-class journey to travel the 59-minute route from London to Weybridge (much quicker than the horse-drawn Royal Mail coach). Although it was a costly mode of transport, the new railway line brought a great change to the life of rural Weybridge, with the influx of wealthy London businessmen and their families. It enabled them to commute every day to their offices in the city and return home by dinner time. The railway made a lasting impression on the district by fuelling a property boom which ultimately led to the break-up of the old estates by speculative property developers. By 1841 Weybridge was one of three intermediate stations at which the Royal Mail train stopped, the others being Kingston (now Surbiton) and Woking Common. The population expanded during the railway years: in 1831 it was 930, in 1851 it had reached 1,200, and by 1891 the figure had risen to 3,944. Although still small, the population had quadrupled in just 60 years.

Weybridge was later connected by a rail link with neighbouring Chertsey and Addlestone, when a branch off the main line was opened in 1848. A bay platform was created at Weybridge to allow the branch line trains to connect with the main line services. The Chertsey line was extended in 1866 to Virginia Water, allowing commuters to travel to London via a different route. A special triangular junction was opened at Weybridge to allow main line trains to join the branch line from both directions. A third railway line was added in 1885, enabling trains to rush through without stopping. Traffic increased so much that in 1902 a fourth line was added, requiring the rebuilding of most of the station buildings, included a new booking hall and office. All traction at this time was by London and South Western Railway (LSWR) steam engines hauling trains made up of short six-wheel based passenger stock. Signalling was by the semaphore system arranged on the block principal. Steam trains continued to operate all services until the line was electrified in 1937 by the addition of a third electrified rail to all the running lines. After this, only long distance trains were steam-hauled, with all commuter journeys handled by the new electrified stock. By this time, the line was run by the Southern Railway, which had been created in 1923 when the Government merged over a hundred private companies into four independent private companies. Nationalisation of the railway network in 1948 did little to affect the service offered. Steam trains continued to run through Weybridge until 1967 when they were withdrawn. Goods traffic declined and the goods yard was closed in 1964. Semaphore signalling was replaced with colour light signals in 1970. A further, unexpected change came on 5 January 1987, when the station booking hall was burnt down by vandals; a new one was subsequently built on the same site. Weybridge was fortunate in that its train service was on a well used commuter route to London and did not suffer the rationalisation and closures caused by the Beeching cuts of the 1960s.

Eight

A Country Retreat

Fanny Kemble, the famous Regency period actress, spent part of her youth in Weybridge in a house called 'Eastlands'. She described Weybridge and district as follows:

> A region of light sandy soil, hiding its agricultural poverty under a royal mantle of gorse and purple heather, with large tracts of blue aromatic pine wood and one or two parts of really fine scenery, where the wild moorland rolls itself up into ridges and rises to crests of considerable height, which command extensive and beautiful views, such as the one from the summit of St George's Hill, near Weybridge.

This rural idyll was soon transformed with the opening of the London and Southampton Railway through Weybridge in May 1838. Wealthy business classes were followed by the middle and later working classes. The main areas of residential development in Weybridge from the 1840s were on Weybridge Heath, the site of the former Oatlands Park estate, the area covered by the Portmore Park estate and, in the early 20th century, on St George's Hill. At first the development took the nature of large country villas and adjoining gardens, and Fanny Kemble described the new developments in Weybridge

39 & 40 Portrait of Fanny Kemble painted by Thomas Sully in 1833 (Courtesy of the Pennsylvania Academy of the Fine Arts), and the rear of Eastlands House from the garden, 1971.

41 The sylvan setting of St George's Hill, Weybridge, *c*.1913. This shows the woods before the area was developed by W.G. Tarrant.

as 'A nest of "villas" made into a suburb of London by the railroads, which intersect in all directions the wild moorland twenty miles from the city (of London), which looked, when I first knew it, as it if might be a hundred.'

Land values in the area in the early 1830s were relatively cheap compared with London, especially as much of the land was of poor quality and was not used for agricultural production. The railway also allowed the bulk movement of goods and materials at a more competitive rate than the canals and waterways, so, with the availability of mass-produced building materials such as bricks, slates, tiles, windows, glass and timber, speculative builders were able to purchase cheap land in the area and build luxury villas for their clients, as well as whole estates and streets of housing for the upper and middle classes who flocked to the area from the 1840s onwards. The builders required a workforce of skilled labourers for the developments, and many more people started their own businesses to service the needs of the growing population.

Weybridge Heath

Before the 1830s the heath area of Weybridge consisted largely of uncultivated land that had been enclosed under the Acts of 1800 and 1811. The land was divided and sold to various landowners, including Robert Bartropp, who purchased land on the northern edge of the heath and at Brooklands in 1811. Robert died in 1839 and his son inherited the estate, selling the land to Sir John Easthope, chairman of the London and Southampton Railway Company, who moved to the area in 1840.

Easthope had been a founding member of the LSRC from 1834, and was involved in the construction of the line when it was cut through Weybridge Heath and St George's Hill. Between 1837-40 he purchased houses and land on the heath, and in 1844 purchased land in the vicinity of the heath from LSRC. Easthope had amassed a fortune of £150,000, mainly through financial speculation, and was a Liberal member of parliament. He was created a Baronet by Lord Melbourne in 1841. He owned a house called

42 Drawing of 'Fir Grove' on Weybridge Heath, from the diary of Rev. Baron, *c.*1865-80. The Rev. Baron was minister of the Congregational Church, Queen's Road.

Firgrove, built before the arrival of the railway. It had been constructed around 1807 by Thomas Liberty, a local builder, and in 1814 Liberty sold the plot of land, including the house, to Captain John Oakes Hardy; it was purchased by the railway company around 1834. The property was expanded by the architect J.B. Papworth, and

Easthope moved in a year later. In 1851 Easthope employed ten labourers to maintain the property and the grounds of 200 acres. In 1854 he sold the house to Albert Wilson. By 1861 Easthope, his wife, and six servants were staying at Firgrove Cottage, which was used as a weekend retreat while he lived at Cumberland Place, London. On Easthope's death in 1865, the estate was sold to Alfred Wilson, and in the 1870s the new owners, the Stone family, sold land for development; 'The Pines' was built on land north of the railway. Afterwards, Firgrove Cottage became known as Firgrove View, and was incorporated into the grounds of a house called Netherfield owned by George Wilson. Firgrove View was demolished around 1924. Firgrove House was renamed Weybridge Towers in 1907 and eventually demolished around 1965.

From the early 1850s Easthope started to sell off his land in the heath area for redevelopment, much of it being purchased by the Wilson family. A house called Bartropps was built on land belonging to Easthope in 1855, followed by Netherfield. This led to the wholesale development of this area of Weybridge. Bartropps was built by William Harrison to a design by Hamilton E. Harwood. Harwood was an architect

43 'Bartropps' on Weybridge Heath, the home of Sir Philip Pilditch, 1903-56. His daughter, May Pilditch, can be seen in the foreground. The photograph was probably taken around 1910.

44 'Firfield House', home of the Cobbett family.

working on railway station designs for the North Midland and South Eastern Railway. Harrison also built Netherfield, on land which he leased to C.H. Parkes. He died in 1879, though his wife continued to live in the area until 1901, in which year Bartropps was sold to Phillip Pilditch, a London architect, who moved there with his family from Kensington, London. The house was extended by the Pilditch family, who added a billiards room, a morning room and servants' quarters. Phillip Pilditch was elected member of parliament for Spelthorne Division of Middlesex in 1918. He retired in 1931, by which time he had been made a Baronet (1929) in honour of his services. He died in 1948, his wife in 1955, and the house was shortly after demolished to make way for a new housing development.

Netherfield House dates from 1869. Charles H. Parkes lived there with his wife and six children and was for many years a parliamentary agent promoting bills for the railway companies. In 1872 he became a director of the Great Eastern Railway, and in 1874 he was made chairman, a post he retained until 1893. Parkes lived at Netherfield in Weybridge until his death in 1895 aged 79 years of age. William Harrison's wife, Eliza, then sold Netherfield to C.H. Ommanney for £7,000. Subsequent

45 The Cobbet family outside their house 'Firfield House' in 1868. Arthur Cobbett is standing with his daughter Amy beside him. Seated left to right in front of them are Edith Cobbett (daughter), Betsey Cobbett (wife), William Cobbett (son), Sarah Anne Cobbett (daughter), and seated on a stool in front of the group is Louise Cobbett (youngest child).

owners of the house include the Baroness de Breyne from 1919-24, Mildred M. Butler, Ernest R. Still and Gouy Dutton. In 1944 it was purchased by Maddine B. Miller and was up for sale again in 1952, advertised for £17,000. The National College of Food Technology purchased it in 1954 and Beecham Products in 1980.

Another important house in this part of Weybridge was Firfield House, built in 1862 for Arthur Cobbett, a high-class grocer and tea merchant. Like many wealthy merchants before him, Cobbett decided to move his family out of London and chose Weybridge. Apart from building a new house, he laid out a croquet lawn and a lawn tennis court. Arthur Cobbett died in 1891, his wife Betsy in 1902. After her death, the family let the house to Alfred Clark. The Cobbett's eldest son, Arthur Rathbone Cobbett, lived at Woburn Chase from 1878; he subsequently sold the family business to the Morrel Brothers. By 1951 Firfield had been converted into flats and by the mid-1950s it was demolished and replaced by houses.

Other lesser houses built in the heath area were constructed on tithe land. Houses built there around 1870 included Croxleys, The Laurels, Woodcote, Noirmont and Firgrove Lodge. Field Place was constructed around 1895 for Henry Yool. Yool was the first Surrey county councillor for Weybridge as well as the vice-chairman of Surrey County Council. He had previously lived at Oakfield. He died in 1894 and a monument was erected in his memory at the top of Monument Hill in 1896 (see p.108).

Heath House was built in 1854 on the northern edge of Weybridge Heath, in the fashionable Italianate style, for Benjamin Scott, who was Chamberlain to the City of London. Scott was involved in the nonconformist movement and in 1863 allowed the Congregational Church to hold services in a building he owned in Heath Road. Mr. and Mrs. Scott died of influenza in London in 1893. By 1919 the house had been converted into a girls' school, known as Heath House School until it closed in 1945, after which it became a hotel. It was saved from demolition in 1987.

The last major house was Foxhill Manor, later called Caenshill, which was built on land on the south-west side of the Heath. It was built in mock-Tudor style in 1900 for Mr. Cox on land purchased from Hugh Locke King of Brooklands in 1897. It was sold in 1912 and purchased by the Locke King family; Dame Ethel Locke King had it remodelled before the First World War, when the house was renamed Caenshill and used as a temporary military hospital. Dame Ethel lived there from 1937 until her death in 1956. The house was saved from demolition in 1995.

Oatlands Park Estate

Fanny Kemble also wrote about the Oatlands Park area during a trip to the village in 1831:

> The beautiful domain of Oatlands was only rented at this time by Lord Francis Egerton, who delighted so much in it that he made overtures for the purchase of it. The house is by no means a good one, though it had been the abode of royalty; but the park is charming.

Later, on Sunday 12 June, she wrote in her journal:

> Its nearly five years since I said my prayers in that dear old little Weybridge church ... We walked on through a part of the park called America because of the magnificent rhododendrons and azaleas and the general wildness of the whole ... It was a beautiful bit of forest scenery; how like America I do not know ...

Lord Egerton lived at Oatlands House until 1844 when he left the property. Edward Hughes Ball Hughes's solicitors put the 875-acre estate up for sale in 1846, dividing it into 64 lots. Oatlands House was sold with 97 acres of land for £11,000 to a Mr. Peppercorn, who sold it in the 1850s to the London and South Western Railway Company, who converted it to a hotel trading under the name of the South Western Hotel Company. The park was then sold off for residential development. The carriageway running through the park was converted into a public road and large villas constructed alongside; this was called Oatlands Drive.

Oatlands Village was built in the 1840s to accommodate the trades people and domestic servants that had arrived in the area to serve the needs of the big houses being built in Oatlands Drive. Communities began to spring up in Anderson Road, built between 1846-59, and St Mary's Road, originally called Ball Road after Mr. Ball, who bought a house nearby. It was renamed St Mary's Road in 1882. By 1859 there were two inns serving the needs of the new

46 'Bramcote', a large villa located off Oatlands Drive, Weybridge, *c.*1870.

47 *Right.* Contemporary print of the *Oatlands Park Hotel*, opened in 1858, and built in the fashionable Italianate architectural style of the time.

48 *Below.* 'Templemere', a large mansion built in Oatlands Park, seen here from the front. The house stood on what is now the corner of Monument Hill and Oatlands Drive, at Temple Market.

populace: the *Flintgate Inn* was on the corner of Oatlands Drive and St Mary's Road, while the *New Inn* was on the corner of Oatlands Drive and Victoria Road. Not everyone liked the intrusion of these watering places and the *New Inn* earned itself such a rowdy reputation that when it came up for sale in 1895 a local resident purchased it to avoid it continuing as an inn, and the licence was sold to an inn opposite Walton railway station. The former *New Inn* was given to the vicar of St Mary's Church as his new home. Templemere estate was another new residential area that grew quickly into a little community. Oatlands Village is unique in keeping its rural charm and character. In 1861 it acquired its own church and school, and in 1869 it became a parish. The area along Oatlands Drive was known for many years as America because of the remark by Fanny Kemble. The name stuck and was even used on official maps until the 1900s.

Portmore Park

In her memoir of the area Fanny Kemble wrote of the

> desolate domain of Portmore Park, its mansion falling into ruin, on one side of it, and on the other the empty house and fine park at Oatlands, the former residence of the duke of York ... The straggling little village lay on the edge of a wild heath and common country.

The present Portmore Park was laid out in the grounds of the old estate after 1887, when Hugh Locke King, son of Peter Locke King of Brooklands, obtained permission to build new roads on the land and sold it off for building development. The main sales of land for redevelopment took place between 1891 and 1901, with houses being built in the area from 1888 until around 1910. The Portmore Park pillars came into the possession of Mr. Ward who had purchased Clinton House in 1882. He

49   Portmore House seen from Church Street in the 1930s. This was the home of Dr. Eric Gardner, the local G.P., who was also the first honorary curator of the Weybridge Museum. The house was originally part of the Portmore Park estate.

50 Boy with horse and cart belonging to the builder, W.G. Tarrant, photographed in 1912.

presented them to the new Urban District Council for Weybridge, formed in 1895; they were to be kept *in situ* at the Thames Street entrance to the estate.

Arthur Rathbone Cobbett, the eldest son of Arthur Cobbett of Firfield House, who had sold the family tea and grocery business in 1887 and received £70,000 for his share of the business, subsequently set himself up as a land speculator and developed the Portmore Park estate and the Quadrant area of Weybridge in the 1890s. He died in 1906, followed by his wife in 1923, after which time their estate was liquidated and the property he acquired was sold off.

St George's Hill, Weybridge

Fanny Kemble's description of St George's Hill, written on 29 May 1831, is worth recording here:

> ... the wooded ranges of St George's Hill, extremely wild and picturesque ... Lord Francis Egerton bought St George's Hill, at the foot of which he built Hatchford, Lady Ellesmere's charming dower house and residence after his death.

Once the Oatlands Park estate was broken up after 1846, the Earl of Ellesmere bought 900 acres on St George's Hill and built a house on its south-western slope. At the same time he began planting trees on what had been a bare hilltop. In the early 1900s the Earl's daughters generously allowed members of the public to use the area for recreational activities.

In 1909 Mr. W.F. Egerton, who owned the freehold to the property, sold some of the land to help offset tax increases introduced by the Liberal government. In 1911 Mr. W.G. Tarrant bought 964 acres from the Egerton family. He was only 36 years old at the time of the purchase and was already a wealthy and well-established businessman, having been involved in the building trade from his youth, running a business from nearby Byfleet. He had a large works manufacturing building materials including wrought iron and leaded lights, a joinery workshop, stone mason's yard, a saw mill and drying sheds. He also owned brickfields at Chobham and Rowlands Castle as well as a couple of plant nurseries at Addlestone and Pyrford. Tarrant's scheme for the hill was an exclusive housing estate for the successful business classes of Edwardian England. The location was ideal for those travelling by train, who could alight at nearby Weybridge railway station, or for those arriving by motor car from London. In 1912 he published his 'Ideal designs for houses to be erected at St George's Hill, Weybridge', following this promotion with another via a special pull-out supplement in the *Surrey Herald* which advertised the types and costs of houses that he planned to build. This brochure praised the beauties of St George's Hill and the surrounding district. Tarrant started building in 1912 and his first thoughts were for an 18-hole golf course as well as a splendid clubhouse, with adjoining tennis courts.

51 'Crow Clump' was typical of the large houses built on St George's Hill by W.G. Tarrant for his clients after 1913. This particular property was built around 1914 for Mr. T.P. Latham, and was designed by the architects Tubbs, Messer and Poulter. It was built in Yaffle Road, previously called Old Avenue, in mellow red brick. Amongst other rooms, it had a billiard room, servants hall, plus 24 bedrooms. As can be seen from the photograph, the garden fell away steeply from the house towards St George's Hill golf course, which was then under construction.

Plans were submitted to Weybridge Council in April 1912 for houses to be built near the main entrance to the hill at the Byfleet Road end. Because the area was also covered by Walton Urban District Council, plans were submitted to them in July 1912 for houses near the top of the hill in present-day Old Avenue. However, before any real progress could be made on developing the hilltop, the First World War broke out, ending all building work for the duration of the war. Instead Tarrant completed some orders from the army for wooden huts for use by the BEF in France, and other war work. Once the war ended work was restarted, and by the early 1920s building was well under way.

Tarrant felt he could repeat the St George's Hill experiment elsewhere. He chose to build a similar estate at Wentworth, near Virginia Water,

which he started in 1923. However, by this time the building industry was affected by a post-war slump which slowed down the demand for large luxury homes on the scale of the developments at St George's Hill. By the early 1930s all orders for Tarrant-built houses had dried up and Tarrant Builders Limited went into receivership after the bank called in the loan.

During the Second World War some of the houses on St George's Hill were converted for military use. Since then more houses have been built, although on a much smaller scale, and the land between the houses has been filled in with new development. However, the exclusive character of the estate survives, very much as it was designed in the early 1900s. Many of the building plans submitted to the local authorities prior to 1920 are deposited with Elmbridge Museum.

Nine

Industrial Weybridge

One of the surprising aspects of the history of Weybridge is the industrial nature of the village over the last three hundred years, especially following the Industrial Revolution of the 18th century, which affected even remote rural communities in Surrey. The industries connected with the village have ranged from milling through to heavy manufacturing at Brooklands. The sad fact is that most of the heavy industrial production has now left the area, particularly over the last thirty years.

In 1961 the Government passed a Factory Act stipulating the health and safety requirements of all employees working in a factory environment. In 1962 50 business premises in Weybridge were being covered by this Act. The list gives a very good insight into the nature of business in the village at the time. The largest employer in the area was Vickers, which ran a huge factory complex on the outskirts of Weybridge at Brooklands. Other businesses included: Kennington Shanks Engineering Company; R.J. Shanks & Co. Ltd. (auto-engineers); J. Burley & Sons Ltd. (agricultural machinery repairs); Thomson & Taylor (Brooklands) Ltd. (general engineers); L. Anstead & Co. Ltd. (sheet metal and oxyacetylene); A. Whittet & Co. Ltd. (oil); Griffin's Garage (auto-repairs); Weybridge Automobiles Ltd. (auto-engines); Albert and Victor Warrington (light engineering); Universal Flaymaster Equipment & Co.; Tilson Metal Fabrications; Wastex, Oil Mills.

52 A postcard of Weybridge Heath.

Other firms were more service oriented, such as Lawes Rabjohns Ltd. (office equipment); George Jarvis and Co. Ltd. (builders); Weyside Cleaners & Furnishers (carpet cleaning); Brooklands Laundry Ltd.; Ketts Radio (T.V. and wireless repairs); Rawlings & Walsh Ltd. (printers); Spring Grove Laundries, and Peto Ross (clothing).

Milling

Ever since the opening of the Wey Navigation from Guildford to Weybridge in 1653, mills have played an important part in the trade of the waterway, although many of the surrounding villages on the Thames, Wey or Mole have had water mills since the Middle Ages. In the area around Weybridge the mills were The Oil Mills on Whittet's Ait, and Coxes Lock Mill, located between Addlestone and Weybridge. Further afield, other mills have existed in Cobham, Byfleet, Esher and on the Ember.

From the 18th century many of these mills were iron-working mills, processing iron ore for use in manufacturing and blacksmithing. Dr. Eric Gardner wrote in 1921 that fires on Weybridge Heath had cleared

> the undergrowth, and revealed a series of more or less parallel trenches, somewhat like the furrows on arable land, but irregular and varying in depths. They are the remains of old iron workings, where ironstone was obtained locally, and although probably no more than about 150 years old, public memory is so short that their nature and origin are almost forgotten.

53 Photograph of Whittet's Oil Mill, 1924.

54 Watercolour of Coxes Lock Mill painted in the 1980s by J. Taylor.

The trenches are strictly limited to the geological formation of the Bagshot Beds, which consists of a lower stratum of Bagshot sand, covered in places by the Bracklesham clay. Between these two strata lies a deposit of ironstone varying from a mere staining of the soil to a definite plate several inches thick; and wherever this ironstone by the conformation of the strata comes within working distance of the surface, there the ground is seamed with trenches, and the ore is found to have been extracted.

This local ironstone only contained about 23 per cent iron ore, and when dug up was conveyed by pack ponies to the various mills in the area for processing; in the Weybridge area it was smelted at the mill on Whittet's Ait, as well as the two mills at Byfleet and one at Downside, Cobham. (An 1803 Act of Parliament refers *inter alia* to an earlier conveyance in 1760 of the two 'iron mills at Byfleet used in the iron and steel manufacture' which, along with their warehouses, yielded a greater annual value than all the manors of Byfleet and Weybridge combined.)

The Weybridge mill was situated at the mouth of the River Wey. Throughout its history the name has changed depending on the owners. Originally known as Ham Haw Mill, it has been known as Thames Lock Mill, Bunn's Iron Mill, Flockton's Mill, Nias Mill, Nias and Whittet's Mill, Whittet's Mill and finally The Oil Mills, Weybridge. It was built on land that once belonged to Chertsey Abbey, and formed part of the boundary lands in A.D. 725. There is no mention of a mill on this site in Domesday Book, although it is probably true that a corn mill was operating near here in the Middle Ages. On a map published by John Senex in 1729 'Weybridge Mill' is marked on the site. On a map of 1732 the plot of ground near the mill buildings is marked as 'Mill Gardens', implying that there was a mill house at that time.

During the 18th century the mill was owned by a Mr. Champain (possibly the husband of the Lady Champain we encountered on p.36, who was robbed by a footpad near Lord Lincoln's Park in 1763) and processed local ironstone. By 1789 the land tax records describe the mill as 'Late Champain'. According to Dr. Eric Gardner, 'Weybridge Mill, also a "Brass Wire Mill" in 1760, had apparently been fitted with machinery to deal with iron by 1779, for a lease of that date prohibits its use for any business that would ... require a great hammer to be worked by water', a proviso inserted in the interest of the owner of the canal, whose water it would use. Shortly after, it passed into the hands of Mr. J. Bunn, who certainly smelted iron there, and in 1812 two trade tokens were issued, the latter having on the obverse a view of the mills with four large chimneys and a waterwheel, inscribed beneath, 'The Weybridge Mills', and on the reverse the legend, 'One Penny payable at Weybridge, I. Bunn and Co'.

However, research has shown that the mill has a much earlier history. It certainly dates back to 1693, when a Robert Douglas built the first mill in Weybridge as a paper mill. The Wey Navigation granted a deed to Douglas on 27 May 1691 to erect Ham Haw Mills. In December 1720 Douglas leased the mill to John Hitchcock; a further lease of 21 years was granted to Hitchcock and William Ockenden by the 2nd Earl of Portmore in 1740, and in August 1761 the Earl of Portmore granted a new 21-year lease to Richard Glover and John Heaton, executors of William Ockenden's estate. On 26 December 1779 Lord Milsington granted a further lease of 21 years to the Hon. Fletcher Norton and James Champain of Weymouth, Dorset.

It is probably the case that when Hitchcock took over in 1720 he converted the mill to iron working, because from 1731 it was known as the 'Iron Mills'. The masters of the mill from 1758 were Captain Fletcher (1758-64), Norton and Champain (1764-73), John Tull (1774-6), Jukes Coulson (1776-95), Jukes Coulson and Co. (1795-1808), and finally John Bunn (1808-17). By 1819 John Bunn had transferred his business to Coxes Lock Mill near Addlestone; thereafter the Weybridge Mill fell into disrepair. The surveyor to the dean and canons of Windsor, who owned the land the mill occupied, wrote in 1820 that:

> The Iron Mills are absolutely nothing more or less than a Heap of Ruins, and so little care is taken that people are continually conveying off the material so that by the end of the existing lease there will scarcely be a vestige of these important Works remaining.

Around 1819 a malt mill, which was possibly hand-operated, was established at Thames Lock House to grind barley and split peas and beans. In 1829, Hamm Court Estate, which was leased by the Earl of Portmore from the dean and canons of Windsor, came up for renewal. The Earl had neglected the estate, and as a result a fine of £1,658 4s. 0d. was imposed on him for compensation. The mill had fallen into such disrepair that the Earl's solicitor, Mr. Scurman, wrote in 1830 requesting permission to pull it down, and the dean and canons had consented. Mr. Scurman wrote to them that, 'I am glad you have consented to let Mr. Gardner remove the Mills which would have been done by Earl Portmore long ago but for the supposition that you might consider him wrong in so doing.'

In 1841 Webster and Thomas Metcalf Flockton of Temperance Mills, Spa Road, Bermondsey, London, negotiated a 21-year lease on the site from 26 March 1842. By June they were in possession and started building a mill for manufacturing oil by crushing seeds. The Flocktons were very poor tenants and abused their position on the Wey Navigation by refusing to pay tolls to Mr. Matthews, the lock-keeper at Thames Lock, using his stables and fencing off his garden without his permission. A lawsuit was filed against them in 1845 and they were found guilty of rebuilding the mill so that it overhung the Wey Navigation and for erecting fences on the towpath obstructing free passage for men and horses. They had also reduced the number of canal gates on the old cut to two, made a new cut under the mill, and erected a flash bar across the canal to hold the water back, thereby flooding the adjoining fields, whose owners subsequently sued the Wey Navigation.

The Flocktons gave up the mill when their lease expired in 1862 and it was transferred to Mr. Nias. Around 1871 he was joined by Mr. A. Whittet, the mill then being known as Nias and Whittet's Oil Mill. They crushed linseed to make cattle-cake. The freehold of the mill was purchased from the dean and canons of Windsor in 1872 for £2,000. Three years later Mr. Nias left the business and Mr. Whittet became sole owner. In 1877 a disastrous fire broke out: barrels of refined oil were rolled into the river for safety, but the heat of the fire burnt the main vats, spilling burning oil into the river and igniting the floating barrels. A huge conflagration ensued which was attended by the fledgling Volunteer Weybridge Fire Brigade.

After the Second World War the mill was made into a limited company and by the 1950s was crushing seeds to extract oil and refining vegetable oils. Another fire broke out in 1959 which damaged part of the building, leaving it a roofless shell. In 1967 the mill, now known as The Oil Mills, Whittet's Ait, was producing oil from copra, ground nuts, cotton seeds, palm kernel, soya beans, rape seeds and linseeds. By 1976 the whole of the island was owned by the Whittet family and the old mill was leased to Wastex Ltd., a waste goods processing company, and other light industry.

Another local mill of great importance was Coxes Lock Mill, on the Wey Navigation, which has probably existed for nearly three hundred years. The first building would have been used for milling silk (the mulberry trees were at Oatlands Palace Gardens). However, the story of the mill really begins in the 1770s, with Alexander Raby, an ironmaster. From 1758 Alexander Raby's father, Edward, controlled the Sussex iron industry at Felbridge. On Edward's death in 1771, Alexander left the family furnace and married Ann Cox. He bought Downside Mill, Cobham, and the two settled nearby. In 1780 he acquired Coxes Lock Mill and local wasteland, thus preventing anyone else setting up in competition. He lived for a while at the old Manor House, Stoke D'Abernon. In 1795 he acquired the Ember Mill at Thames

Ditton, by which time he had a large iron-smelting empire, with sites in Wales, Derbyshire and Surrey, but during 1808-9 he liquidated his company, selling all his Surrey holdings, and he ended life dependent on charity.

In 1813 John Taylor purchased the mill; it then passed to William Thompson. On 12 January 1819 the mill was acquired by John Bunn, after he had given up the Weybridge Mill. The deeds indicate that, apart from the mill itself, there were also mill cottages and a stable block. In 1829 the mill was converted to a flour mill, because the Surrey iron business had collapsed. It then passed to Daniel Lambert, who improved the premises; in 1867 the mill had five pairs of French burr grinding stones. But Lambert died in 1867, leaving the mill to his son, Benjamin, who leased it to Henry R. Pery of Addlestone. By 1878 the mill was leased to Lorenzo George Dundas, Lieutenant-Colonel of Addlestone. From 1887 it was in the hands of R. & H. Adams, and was managed by A.E. Humphries and E.H. Gale. In the 1890s the water wheel was replaced by a 40 h.p. turbine and new equipment was installed, including a new roller plant, and in 1904 the mill became The Coxes Lock Milling Company Limited, with Humphries as the managing director and Gale as the company secretary.

Between 1901-7 various expensive improvements were made to the mill, including the building of a new 5,000 qr. grain silo, as well as a 15 sack plant and a 300 h.p. Wood-House and Mitchell steam engine. Mr. Humphries died in 1935 and the mill was managed by Mr. Gale until his death in 1940 after 53 years' service at the mill. One employee, Mr. Walter White, was at the mill from 1894 until he retired in the 1950s. Mr. Humphries' sons recalled that during the 1880s the Mill House was rented by Commie-Gilchrist, the famous music hall actress. By the 1960s the mill was in the hands of the Associated British Food Group, and the manager was Gilbert Gale. The mill was finally closed in April 1983, putting 55 people out of work, by the then owners Allied Mills Ltd., who owned a total of 20 mills around the country at that time.

Breweries

The Old Brew House in Weybridge, which was located by Church Walk, between Jessamy Road and Radnor Road, was pulled down in 1906. Originally it was part of a brewery that had existed in the village since the 1650s and may have been run by the Elmer family. Tradition has it that the men who operated the barges going up and down the river used to stop at the Weybridge Quay and rest themselves in the forecourt of the Old Brew House sipping beer and smoking their clay pipes. A brewery has existed in Weybridge since the 1400s because there are numerous references in the Court Rolls of the Manor of Weybridge to brewers constantly being prosecuted for selling beer by the draught instead of by the measure, as they were supposed to do.

Boots and Shoes

In the days before mass-produced shoes every village had at least one boot and shoemaker. Their products were hand-crafted using traditional materials, and lasted a long time, as they were constantly repaired. However, the cost for a pair of new shoes or boots was as high as a week's salary for a labourer.

Elmbridge Museum has in its collection a lap-stone and riding boot made by 'Hone Cobbler of Weybridge' in 1812. James Hone was born c.1784 and died in 1850. He had a son, also called James, who was born in Weybridge in 1827. James married in 1862 and had a son called Herbert, born in the same year. James was also a cobbler, working in Weybridge. His grandfather had a sister, who had an illegitimate child called Alfred, who had a cobbler's shop at the foot of Monument Hill in 1865, and later in Baker Street in 1886.

Many other family-run boot and shoe repair businesses operated in the area, such as the Foot family, who had a shop in Church Street in 1896-7. The business was operated by Joseph Henry Foot with his wife Elizabeth. They had three children, the youngest of whom was baby daughter Florence Maria Foot; the others were Daisy Foot and Herbert William Joseph Foot. Elliott and Wade were also boot and shoe repairers in the 1900s.

55 The Foot family and customers standing outside Foots' Cobblers shop in Church Street in 1896. Joseph Henry Foot is standing in the middle with a white apron, to his right is Elizabeth Foot, his wife, holding baby Florence Maria Foot. In the front row is, to the left, Daisy Mary Foot, with her brother Herbert William Joseph Foot.

Coachbuilders

The Puttock family of Weybridge were carriage builders from the early 19th century. They had premises at 41 High Street, now the site of Gascoigne Pees/Black Horse Agency. David Puttock, the founder of the business, was born in 1808 and died in 1883. In 1830 he was living in Chertsey and moved to Weybridge around

1841. A wheelwright by trade, he was married to Jane Puttock, by whom he had five children. The High Street premises were originally part of Orchard House, which occupied land between Baker Street and the High Street. The house was demolished around 1816, and replaced by three cottages, part of which survived until 1976 as 'Robin's Nest'. In 1867 David Puttock is described as the yearly tenant of the property, which he shared with a Mr. Marnier.

In May 1868 the property bordering the High Street was sold at auction at *The Ship Inn* for £4,600, the Puttocks' house being sold for £730. This led to the further development of Weybridge High Street, when 158 feet of land was sold to build cottages. The census returns for 1881 list the family as David Puttock, head of family and 'coachbuilder', 71 years of age, with his wife Ellen Puttock, 47 years of age. Elizabeth Puttock also lived there and was listed as a 'servant'. The Puttock family home is described as having a flower garden, orchard, a smithy, painter's shop and a loft. David died, leaving his two sons, Alfred and Richard, to take over the business. By 1913 the business was registered under the name of Mrs. Emily Puttock. The frontage onto the High Street was originally 107 feet long, but this was gradually whittled down as the land fronting the High Street was

56 Puttock's coachbuilding works facing onto the High Street, *c*.1900.

57 Newman's corn and seed merchants premises on the corner of the junction of Baker Street and the High Street in 1890.

sold off for development. There were inscriptions over the entrance to the premises which read 'Carriage-Puttock-Factory', and 'Smith Work and General'.

Boat builders

One trade of obvious importance to a village so close to the Wey Navigation was the boat-building industry. Weybridge Marine were a prominent company. Mr. Tappin, a former employee, remembered the various boat-building companies along the Thames and Wey:

> There were many boat builders and repair yards along the river. The Duntons owned several—the main yard being on the Shepperton bank. They also had a boathouse on the Weybridge bank that is now the Ladies Rowing Club's Headquarters. Another well-known local boat builder was Harris. He owned the boatyard, now Weybridge Marine, after Keene and before Tappin. Eventually he became a bigger boat builder than Dunton, and bought up some of his yards. At one time Harris owned 300 skiffs, punts and canoes. The *Lincoln Arms* was also at one time

known as *Harris's Hotel*. The men who worked in the boatyards were journeymen boat builders; they moved around the different yards to work on the boats and would think nothing of cycling 50 miles along the river to work. One of Dunton's men used to cycle from Wargrave, near Henley, every day.

The Holstein Printing Works

Holstein House was situated in the High Street, and was built by the 2nd Earl of Portmore in the mid-18th century. The name is believed to originate from Frederick Christian, Prince of Holstein, who is said to have lived in the building in the 18th century. The property was certainly empty by 1787, and little is known of it until 1796 when it was occupied by the Earl of Cavan. In 1800, Sir Richard Onslow acquired the property. In 1806 it was occupied by six London booksellers, who had combined their resources to set up a printing company, in which they had invested £4,000 on a 21-year lease. Joseph Johnson (1758-1809) was the founder of the business and was instrumental in helping to organise the London book trade. In 1807

58 A watercolour of the rear of Holstein House painted *c.*1830 by T.G. Worthington.

R. Faulder, a bookseller, leased Holstein House to him and his company of London booksellers. He had 12 printing presses installed and a Samuel Hamilton was employed as the printer. Hamilton ran the business for the partners, his own printing business in Falcon Court, London, having been destroyed by fire in 1803. The Weybridge business must have been the largest print works in Surrey at the time. The aim of the partners was to print affordable books which would have a wide appeal. Unfortunately, Johnson did not live long enough to see the firm established as he died in 1809. By 1812 Hamilton had acquired the plant and its premises, running the business as his own, until he left Weybridge in 1818. Charles Worthington owned the premises from 1818-9, after which time the works ceased to exist. Elmbridge Museum has a number of the books printed at the works, including *The Vicar of Wakefield* by Goldsmith, *The Iliad* translated by Alexander Pope, *The Poetical Works of Alexander Pope, Esq.*, *Poems* by William Cowper and *Rosabella; or a mother's marriage, Vols.I-V.*

Gordon Watney's Black Boy Works

In neighbouring Addlestone was a factory run by Major Gordon Watney. He had originally established a motor works in Weybridge in 1911, when he started repairing Mercedes motor cars at South Lodge in March Road, but local residents complained of the noise and forced Watney to look for alternative accommodation. He subsequently purchased land on the corner of Weybridge Road and Ham Moor Lane. By 1912 the company had a new repair shop and was employing about 25 workers.

At the outbreak of the First World War Watney moved the factory over to war production, manufacturing munitions. New buildings had to be constructed to house the enlarged workforce, now 500 people. In 1915 he started his own military unit, known locally as 'The Watney Column' or 'The Watney Lot'. These were skilled mechanics and fitters who formed an army unit known as 244 Motorised Transport Company, Royal Army Service Corps. They served in the Balkans from 1916-19, providing motorised transport for the British Army who were helping the Serbian Army fight the Germans and Austrians.

As the same time the works was used to repair 120 h.p and 160 h.p. Beardmore engines used in FE2B aeroplanes fighting on the Western Front. Watney's also made Clerget Rotary Seven Cylinder engines. These were tested on a bench at the rear of the works, where eight aero engines were run for eight hours apiece, emitting a terrible noise in the process. This obviously annoyed the local inhabitants no end, because the testing continued both day and night. Also tested were Siddeley-Puma engines, Hispano-Suiza engines and BR2 engines. The works consisted of two fitting shops, a machine shop, central stores, a test bench, offices, a blacksmith's forge, garages for lorries and a medical centre. There was also an Aeronautical Inspectorate Department at the factory. In 1918 a fire devastated the works, destroying many buildings. King George V and Queen Mary visited the factory in that year in recognition of the good work done there during the course of the war.

During the First World War the Weybridge Operatic Society and St James's School both used a hall in the factory for staging performances. In 1919 the Anglo-American Oil Company (now Esso Petroleum) purchased the firm, which was reborn as The Weybridge Motor Engineering Company, repairing all the motorised vehicles belonging to the oil company. At this time the works was known as 'The Black Boy Works'. In 1935-6 the company went into voluntary liquidation.

Bleriot

The French aircraft manufacturer Spad was formed in 1910 by Armand Deperdussin as the Société Pour Les Appareils Deperdussin. By 1914 the company was in financial difficulty and sold out to Bleriot, the company started by Louis Bleriot, the pioneering French aviator who flew across the English Channel in 1909.

In 1916 the Royal Aircraft Factory designed the SE5 biplane for use on the Western Front which was powered by a 200 h.p. geared Hispano-Suiza engine. The Royal Aircraft Factory placed an order in February 1917 for the production of 400 such aircraft, the work to be shared between Martynside Limited and Vickers Limited, at Brooklands, Weybridge. In July a further order for 850 aircraft was placed with the Bleriot and Spad works at Addlestone and with Vickers. The Bleriot and Spad works at Addlestone later became the Air Navigation Company Limited.

Lang Propeller Works

Lang Propellor Works was located at the Riverside Propeller Works, near the junction of the Thames and Wey, on the island now known as Whittet's Ait. The company was founded by A.A. Dashwood Lang, who patented a design for a propeller in 1911, having joined the Bristol Aviation Company as their chief propeller expert. However, by 1913 he had founded the Lang Propeller Company in Weybridge, where there was already a substantial amount of aircraft activity. At the outbreak of the First World War there was a huge demand for wooden propellers and by the early months of the war he was employing a large workforce at Weybridge.

The propellers were not made out of solid pieces, but were built up from layers of laminated wood then glued into position and shaped and finished by hand. Once the required shape had been defined, the whole assemblage was roughed down by hand, sandpapered, polished and varnished. Propellers were made during the First World War for all manner of aircraft, including the huge 16-ft. diameter, four-bladed propellers used on airships, made up from 16 laminated sheets. Propellers intended for use on seaplanes often had their leading edge sheathed in copper to protect it against the effects of water damage.

59 A group of factory workers employed at the Bleriot Factory, Addlestone, 1915.

Vickers

Perhaps the most important industry in Weybridge has been Vickers, who began manufacturing aeroplanes at Brooklands in 1911. Hugh Fortescue Locke King, who owned much of the land in and around Weybridge, decided in 1906-7 to pay for the construction of a purpose-built race track on his land at Brooklands. This was the very first racing car circuit in the country, a vast concrete track measuring nearly three miles. Steeply banked curves allowed the primitive racing cars of the Edwardian era to go flat out without having to brake. The track took 18 months to build, at a cost of £150,000, and was officially opened on 17 June 1907, the first race taking place on 6 July.

Vickers began in Sheffield in 1908, when it was commissioned by the Government to manufacture an airship for the Admiralty. Though not a success, this was their first attempt at powered flight. In 1912 they started a flying school at Brooklands and in 1915 an aircraft manufacturing department. From 1919 a design team was also established at Brooklands. The first aircraft produced was the BE2c biplane designed by the Royal Aircraft Factory at Farnborough, and 75 of these were built at Brooklands during 1915-16. Of the SE5 biplane built to combat the Zeppelin threat, 1,650 were produced. The FB5 Gunbus (designed with mountings for machine guns) and the Vickers Vimy bombers were also built there during the First World War. The factory became famous during the Second World War, being one of the sites responsible for the construction of the Wellington bomber; 2,514 were built at Brooklands out of a total of 11,461 produced

nationally. In the post-war period Vickers concentrated on building civilian commercial aircraft from the Viking VC1 through to the successful VC10 series of jetliners.

The Brooklands site also attracted the attention of aviation pioneers Alliott Verdon Roe, Tommy Sopwith and Harry Hawker. Sopwith learned to fly at Brooklands in 1910 and started his own flying school there in 1912, as well as building his own aircraft. He linked up with the Australian Harry Hawker in 1914 to form the Sopwith Aviation Company, purchasing premises in nearby Kingston upon Thames. The company built the famous Sopwith Pup fighter during the First World War, but at the end of the war it went into decline and eventual receivership in 1920. The company was reformed as the H.G. Hawker Engineering Company and in the 1930s it designed and built the Hawker Hurricane fighter aircraft, first flown from Brooklands on 6 November 1935.

Hawker-Siddeley and Vickers were nationalised and merged in 1977 to form British Aerospace, which was later privatised. However, in 1986 British Aerospace were cutting costs and eventually implemented a phased run-down of their Weybridge plant. Closure came in 1988 and nearly 4,000 employees lost their jobs. Fortunately, some were saved and staff transferred to the military aircraft factory at Kingston upon Thames, but this too closed four years later in 1992. The Kingston factory was where the Harrier Jump Jet and the Hawk Fighter were designed and built. The demise of the aircraft factory in 1988 and the redundancy of so many people had a great impact on the economy of Weybridge and the surrounding towns and villages.

Ten

Inns and Taverns

Another surprising aspect of the village's history is the sheer number of public houses in the area given the relatively small population. In the early 20th century there were at least 16 public houses and hotels in Weybridge village serving food and drink. Of these, nine were in existence in the 18th century; a further seven were built in the 19th century to serve the requirements of the expanding village. Many of these were used by travellers as stopping off points on their journeys. Some of them, like *The Ship Inn*, became staging posts for coaches to change horses and for passengers to obtain refreshment.

The Old Crown

This is the third public house located in the vicinity of Thames Street, and was probably used by the bargees working on the nearby Wey Navigation. It is a typical Surrey building, with weather-boarding on the exterior giving a very pleasant appearance, and is a grade II listed building. The earliest reference to the oldest Weybridge pubs is in the Petty Sessions records of *c*.1729. Until 1832 this was known as *The Crown* public house, but thereafter it has been called *The Old Crown*.

The Duke of Newcastle owned the inn in 1782. In 1788 the Duke of York acquired it

60 Pen and ink drawing of *The Old Crown*, Thames Street, 1942.

when he purchased the whole of the Oatlands Park estate. In 1822 the Duke sold the inn at a public auction to James Dryer of Tooks Court, Chancery, London. The original sale document describes the inn thus:

> The Crown Public House with stabling and a large room next the river, and three cottages with garden in the occupation of Messrs. Gale, Wells and Aslett, but the whole on lease to Mr. Hall, for an unexpired term of 12 years and a quarter, from midsummer 1822, at a very low rent of only £21 per annum which may be very considerably increased on the expiration of the lease.

The inn was later purchased by W.S. & C.D. Hodgson, who became the famous Hodgson's Kingston Breweries Ltd. in 1886. Courage purchased the building in the 1970s.

The King's Arms

This building was modern, having been erected on the site of a much earlier inn in the late 1930s. The original inn was probably an 18th-century building which had an upper floor added in the 19th century. The village pound for stray animals stood opposite the inn. William Baker was the mid-18th century publican until he died in 1770 and the business was inherited by his daughter, Mary Keene, who had married Daniel Keene of Shepperton. Mary died in 1775 and the Keene family sold the business to Thomas Cooper in 1789, who was a Walton-on-Thames brewer. Both the Keenes are buried in a vault in the graveyard of St James's parish church. In 1812 the Cooper family sold the inn to Robert Whitburn, a brewer from Ripley. Farnell Brewery at Isleworth acquired the business in 1828, which then became part of the Isleworth Brewery Company. One local family that had a long connection with *The King's Arms* was the Matthews family, who were in residence there from 1867 until 1930.

In 1981 *The King's Arms* was renamed the *Farnell Arms*, but the public house closed in 1997 and a small estate, consisting of four terraced three-storey town houses and a three-storey block of flats, was built on the site. The last publican was Mr. Himpfen, who had been landlord since 1980.

The Lincoln Arms

Situated at the northern end of Thames Street, this inn faces onto the Wey at the junction with the Thames. It is one of the oldest in Weybridge, and derives its name from the Earls of Lincoln who owned nearby Oatlands Park. Benjamin Jacob was the innkeeper when the building was known as *The Row Barge*. In 1780 it was known as *The Anchor and Lincoln Arms* and in 1826 as *The Anchor*. Documents from 1824 and 1840, however, show that it reverted to its previous name, although since the 1840s it has been known as *The Lincoln Arms*. John Hartwell of Wandsworth, London sold it to Joseph Hall of Weybridge for £400 in 1791. William Harris, a Staines brewer, bought the inn in 1819, and on his death the property was sold to William Lewis Harris, a brewer of Weybridge. He bought it at an auction at *The Queen's Head*, Weybridge on 19 February 1833. Seven years later the inn was again sold, to another brewer, this time William Holland of Godalming. He sold it for £1,850 to Richard Whitbourne, also of Godalming, in 1848. In 1866 William Shaw of Shepperton Manor purchased the inn. The innkeeper at this time was Richard Harris, who had acquired the lease in 1845; it was to remain in the Harris family until 1884.

The Ship

This is perhaps the best known of all the public houses in the village. Cockfighting is said to have taken place here. John Dryland was the first licensee of the inn, when it was known as *The Anchor*. In 1780 it was owned by Sarah Brown and occupied by Widow Edgell, who changed the name in 1793 to *The Ship*. During the Napoleonic Wars a room was kept at the inn for recruiting men, especially during the invasion scare of 1803. A poster was issued with the following:

> MEN OF WEYBRIDGE! I am authorised by the Lord-Lieutenant of this County to address you ... I have applied for the honour of commanding those Men in this Parish and its Vicinity, who will come voluntarily forward to learn the use of Arms, William Barnett, Weybridge, August 5th, 1803. A BOOK remains open, at the SHIP INN,

WEYBRIDGE, to receive the Names of those Men who will join me in learning the USE of ARMS.

For much of its life *The Ship* was used as a coaching inn. In 1839 a coach called *The Sovereign* stopped at *The Ship* at 8.15 in the morning on its way from Addlestone to London. The return journey started from *The Bolt and Tun* in Fleet Street, London, at 3.30 p.m. and arrived at *The Ship* at 7.15 p.m.

The Queen's Head

Built on the south side of Bridge Street near Heath Road, in The Quadrant area of Weybridge, the inn is situated at the western end of the village. A daily coach used to run from the inn, calling every morning during the summer at 8 a.m. and 9 a.m. in the winter. Innkeepers included John Keene (1838-45), Thomas Armstrong (1855), who was also a brickmaker, and Henry and Martha Marshall (1862-78).

The Portmore Arms

This was the first inn called *The Portmore Arms*, and occupied part of present-day Portmore House, opposite St James's Church in Church Street; it was closed *c*.1832. The Sun Fire Insurance register entry for 1749, for 'Richard Stamford at the *Anchor* and *Lord Portsmouth's Arms Inn* in Weybridge in the County of Surrey, innholder', almost certainly refers to *The Portmore Arms*, which was described as a brick and tiled building with an insurance value of £300, Hunt, Dawson, Todd and Miller, occupiers. From about 1832-5 the inn was let out as private houses. However, around 1869 a *Portmore Arms* public house had reappeared in the village where Thames Street joins Beale's Lane. The inn finally closed around 1885.

The Three Tuns

Another inn that no longer exists is *The Three Tuns*, once located in Thames Street near Jessamy Road. The first mention of it is from around 1826 when it was owned by Joseph Hall, with Thomas Watson as the tenant; the last innkeeper was William Robert in 1862, and the inn appears to have closed around 1865.

The Stag and Hounds

Before Oatlands Park was broken up in 1846, this inn would have been near the main gate of the estate, and it was ideally situated near the cricket ground on the common. The earliest

61 *The Stag and Hounds*, Hanger Hill in the 1920s. At the time of writing this public house is an Italian restaurant called 'Caffe Uno'.

mention of the inn is in the Byfleet manorial records of 1751, when it had a rent of 6d. In 1809 the inn was sold at an auction held at *The Anchor Inn*, Shepperton, and Mr. Joseph Hall of Weybridge bought the premises. From 1809-19 the inn had several different names, including *The Hare and Hounds*. The Harris family purchased the freehold in 1849 from the lord of the manor, Edward Hughes Ball Hughes. By 1997 the public house had been converted into an Italian restaurant, called The Caffe Uno.

The Newcastle Arms

Built in Church Street at the very heart of Weybridge, the name of this inn originated from Henry Clinton, the 9th Earl of Lincoln, who was also the Duke of Newcastle-under-Lyme, *c*.1768. The Hand-in-Hand Friendly Society regularly met in the inn between 1779-94.

It was the receiving house for mail in Weybridge between 1828-32. The letters arrived by cart every morning at 9 a.m. and were collected at 4 p.m. every afternoon.

The Hand and Spear

The development of *The Hand and Spear*, at The Heath, was due to its proximity to the new London and Southampton railway. Built by the Locke King family on their own land, it is an imposing brick building in the Italianate style so popular in the mid-19th century, with a four-storey tower that dominates the whole building. The name is derived from the Locke King coat-of-arms, which shows a hand holding a broken spear shaft. At the time of its opening in 1839 it was managed by J. Featherstone, and at this time was a posting house.

62 *The Newcastle Arms* after a fire had gutted the Howard's fish shop, which was located next door, *c*.1900. Firemen Alden and Collyer from the Weybridge Fire Brigade are shown in the photograph. The sign board for the inn records that B. Mills was the licensee. A board for T. Kirk, Fly Proprietor, advertises Hansom cabs and carriages for hire.

63 Lithographic print of *The Hand and Spear Hotel*, drawn by G.F. Prosser in the 1840s.

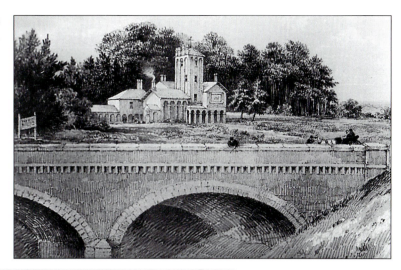

64 *The Grotto Inn* on Monument Hill, *c.*1908.

The Locke King family, who lived at nearby Brooklands House from 1860-1936, used *The Hand and Spear* to entertain their guests who arrived by rail from London. After the building of the Brooklands race track in 1907, the inn was used by racing drivers as a convenient place to stay; Sir Malcolm Campbell and John Cobb were among the guests. The grade II listed building was purchased by the Allied Domecq Leisure Group in 1996 and several internal alterations were made, including bricking up windows, removing a fireplace and knocking down part of a wall. There was local outrage in 1997 when the owners changed the name to *The Formula and Firkin*, although the legend *The Hand and Spear* is still retained on the outside wall.

The Grotto

This public house was located at the junction of Baker Street and Monument Hill, and began life as a beer house around 1839. The name of the inn is obviously taken from the Grotto that was built at Oatlands in the 18th century and demolished in 1948. A sale catalogue, issued in 1869 by Waterer and Son for an auction held at *The Ship* hotel, announces the sale of 'an old-established freehold beer house known as *The Grotto* most advantageously situate at the junction of two important thoroughfares, near the entrance to Oatlands Park'. Around 1900 the building was rebuilt in a mock-Tudor style with gables and beams.

65   The pub garden at the rear of *The Mitre* inn located on Heath Road.

The Mitre

Situated in Heath Road, halfway between Weybridge village and the railway station, this inn was built *c.*1860. In 1904 Hodgsons Brewery at Kingston leased the premises, purchasing it from the will of Mrs. Eliza Lord in 1912. Courage Breweries later bought it from Hodgsons.

The Greyhound

This inn was built in Princes Road around 1867 on land purchased from Evan Hare in 1865. Brandon's Putney Brewery bought it and later sold the business to Mann, Grossman and Paulin.

The Jolly Farmer

A mid-19th-century building situated in Princes Road, this was converted in 1870 to a beer house.

The British Volunteer

The name of this inn at Heath Road is owing to the revival of the volunteer army movement in the 1860s. The inn was built *c.*1870 on copy-hold land owned by Thomas Harrison.

The Duke of York

An inn was built here around 1860-70 in Queen's Road after the break-up of the Oatlands Park estate from 1846. The name comes from the former owner of the estate. The present building dates from the 1920s.

Eleven

Street Scenes

Rawlings Directory for the year 1897 describes Weybridge as follows:

Weybridge is the one place in the district where progress and development are particularly noticeable. The year 1897 has seen a steady increase in the number of houses and shops there. The larger dwellings, in the more rural parts of the village, have not, perhaps, grown to any appreciable extent, but they appear to be continuously occupied, notwithstanding the onward march of progress is calculated to destroy some of the rural charms. From a business point of view, however, the greatest improvement is observable. In the first place the London and County Banking Company have removed from their small unsuitable premises in Church Street to an imposing building which they had erected at the junction of High-street and Baker-street, which is a distinct ornament, and an improvement upon the squalid tumbledown shanties, which previously occupied the site upon which the bank now stands. Then again, a great alteration has been made at the entrance to the village from Addlestone where a large house and grounds have been transformed into a row of fine handsome shops, known as The Quadrant. Two of these shops are already occupied, respectively by Mr. Thomas Dix as a pork butcher's, and Mr. G. Gates as a fishmonger's and poulterer's; whilst the others are not likely to remain unoccupied for any length of time.

66 Watercolour of the shops on the corner of Baker Street and the High Street, painted by Henry Stage in 1920.

67 Watercolour view of no. 66 Baker Street, painted in 1950.

68 Photograph of Howard & Sons fish shop in Church Street, 1920s.

One of the most distinguished streets in Weybridge is Baker Street, which has a long and interesting history. It has had several names down the years and until 1800 was known as Loom Pit Lane. After 1804 the name was changed to Shelton Lane, then Back Street, and finally Baker Street. According to local tradition it was named

after a baker's shop at the town end of the street which opened on Sundays so that villagers could put their roast into the baker's ovens to cook while they were attending church.

Local traders have always given the street the friendly atmosphere for which it is renowned. A lady's black and white jacket that was made just before the First World War was given to the museum in 1973 from the estate of a Mrs. Gordon, whose family had a drapery business in Baker Street. Alfred Bannister first opened his draper's shop in Baker Street in the early 1900s and prided himself on providing fashionable clothing for wealthy local ladies.

Until the late Victorian period there were few houses in Baker Street, apart from the junctions with High Street and Church Street. Cottages did exist in the street, but they were relatively small affairs. No. 66 at the Loom Pit Lane (now known as Baker Street) end of Love Lane, opposite St James' School, was the home of the Luxford family, the Weybridge removal firm. The property originally belonged to Lady Dorotha Tuite who owned the house in 1801. After the enclosures of the early 19th century Lady Tuite owned property in Weybridge, and five acres in Byfleet. She later exchanged her land in Byfleet for four more acres in Weybridge bordered by Loom Pit Lane, High Street and Bell Lane. Her husband, Sir Henry Tuite, Bt., owned 17 houses in Weybridge in 1804, of which only seven were occupied. The Luxford family purchased No. 66 and continued to live there until 1984, when the house was sold to the Berkeley Property Group for redevelopment. A new building, in the old style, was built on the site in 1987.

William Howard had a fishmonger's shop at No. 7 Baker Street from about 1870. A photograph of 1880 shows him standing outside his 18th-century shop. From the 1890s the premises became an estate agent's and in 1903 an auctioneer's owned by John Bower Binns, which it has been ever since. The family shop moved to Church Street

Where the National Westminster bank stands today, on the corner of Baker Street and High Street, stood a dwelling belonging to William Newman, who in 1849 established a

Corn, Coal and Coke merchant's business. This was demolished to make way for the bank, which opened in 1897. The Newman family are famous in Weybridge for their long association with the trade in coal and corn. William Newman was born in Southampton in 1822, and soon afterwards his parents moved to Weybridge. The family traded in agricultural produce from their shop at Baker Street Cottage. They sold hay, dog biscuits, cattle food and general goods. William's son, Walter, married Mary Anne Mingay on 2 March 1881, and lived in Baker Street until 1897, when they sold the cottage to the London and County Banking Company (later the National Westminster Bank).

Walter moved to 1 Dorset Villas, Weybridge, which later became part of Dorchester Road. Walter's son, Arthur, born in 1887, later lived at 2 Dorchester Road,

Weybridge. Arthur was responsible for restarting the family business in the 1920s after it had lapsed in the early 1900s. His brother, Frank, took over the business in 1926. In the 1950s the family sold the business to Pyle of Addlestone. They had been trading in Weybridge for just over one hundred years. Elmbridge Museum has a number of artefacts relating to the Newman family including a shop signboard.

Minorca House, off Church Street, was bought by Lord Milsington, eldest son of the 3rd Earl of Portmore, for his mistress, Frances Murrells. Lord Milsington's wife, Mary Elizabeth, died in 1797 and soon after Lord Milsington married Frances. They had no children and the title died out. The house was pulled down about the time of Queen Victoria's Diamond Jubilee; Queen's Parade was built in its place and Minorca Road was laid out.

69 Minorca House in the 1860s.

Two other houses of distinction were Hayes House and Pyrcroft (mentioned in the Cromwellian Survey of 1650). Pyrcroft had 79 acres of grounds. Other houses in Church Street include The Old House, once owned by Captain Groves who had fought with the Duke of Marlborough. He is reputed to have drunk six bottles of wine a day, his servants disposing of the empty bottles in the River Wey until the vestry found out and ordered them to stop. Elm Lodge was built on land once occupied by a farmhouse of 1478 belonging to Robert Hacche. Nutfield is another important house, having been the one time home of Sarah Taylor (1793-1867), who in 1820 married John Austin (1790-1859).

The Antiques Shop in Church Street, opposite the parish church, was owned in 1856 by the Cooper family, who made straw hats and bonnets; they also kept the only grocery store in Weybridge. Mr. Cooper wore a top hat while making deliveries and sold bulls' eyes, cough sweets and, at Christmas, 'white mice' to the local children. A family called the Gems owned the shop in 1905 and advertised 'China and Glass Riveted, at 2d. a rivet'; at the time it was known as the Olde Curiosity Shoppe. Another shop, No. 16 Church Street, was used in the late 19th century as a chemist's shop; the occupant from 1894-7 was Mr. F. Harvey; from 1897-1900, Mr. C.W. Austin; from 1900-1, Mr. A.E. Wilson, and from 1902-23, Mr. Nethercoat. The Martins had the

premises from 1923-68 and from 1968-75 it was a greengrocer's. It became the Riverside Chinese Take-Away in 1976.

Church Street also had a very well-known butcher by the name of Thomas Dix. An article in the *Surrey Herald* for 1936 says:

> In 1836 the business was opened in Heath Road by Robert Dix at what is now Elm Lodge and then transferred to the present premises in Church Street which had previously been a private school attended by Thomas Dix, who succeeded his father in the management of the business under the style of Thos. Dix. The business went steadily on until it was joined in 1896 by G. Gillingham, the father of the present managing director, who entered into partnership on the ending of his war service. In 1914 a shop was opened in Queen's Road for the customers of that district.

In 1933 Percy Gillingham joined the family business and when his father died in 1937 took over; he sold the business in about 1951. By 1971 the site had been redeveloped, with new shops replacing the family store.

One of the most popular and fondly remembered shops in Weybridge was at 68 Church Street. Madeley's was managed by John Tollow, a nephew of the proprietor. The original shop had been rather a dilapidated affair, but it was replaced by a new shop designed in 1891 by

70 Postcard of Thomas Dix's butcher's shop in Church Street, showing the shop canopy with carcasses hung beneath it and Mr. Dix and his assistant standing beside the display, *c*.1900.

71 Madeley's shop in the High Street with *The Newcastle Arms* just visible on the left, *c.*1890. The shop is double-fronted with a wide variety of produce on display including groceries and general provisions, as well as a pig's carcass hanging in the doorway. Two members of the shop staff pose outside the shop for the photographer, along with horse-drawn delivery carts. A delivery boy can be seen holding his hand cart with the legend 'Madeley, Weybridge' printed on its side. The shop had a stable block and yard, located on the right of the photograph, where the horse and cart could be stored when out of use.

a young local architect, Lindus Forge, after the earlier shop had burnt down in a fire. John Tollow died in 1916 aged 53 years of age. Sainsburys bought the shop in 1920 and remodelled it in 1922. They continued to trade until the shop closed on 5 May 1973. It was remarkable for its lavish interior, wooden fittings and Art Nouveau floor and wall tiles. Another well-known shop since closed down was Haslett's women's clothes shop, which was situated on the corner of Church Street and Balfour Road. The shop had traded in Weybridge for 150 years, run by three generations of the Haslett family until it was taken over by the Bakers in the 1920s.

The High Street in Weybridge has been a major thoroughfare since the 18th and early 19th centuries, with a wide variety of shops. For many years it was dominated by Holstein Hall, which was built in the grounds of Holstein House in 1904 by Mr. John Wiltshire. The Hall was a prominent feature in the life of the village for 60 years. It was used as a public hall until 1917,

when it was taken over by Vickers for aircraft production. It had various owners until Samuel Howard Wood acquired it in 1923 for a motor car showroom, which opened in 1924. After the death of Mr. Wood in 1927 the business continued in the family until 1963, when the building was demolished and replaced by a modern parade of shops.

Other shops included Elliot and Wade, boot and shoe maker's, as well as 'The Hut' refreshment rooms run by the Crocker sisters. The Weybridge post office opened here in 1914 to replace the earlier post office in Heath Road. A telephone exchange was added in 1929. Tappin Brothers operated a grocery business from 52 High Street from 1897. A. Lock & Sons operated from the same premises in 1909, selling market garden produce.

The 1922-3 *Kelly's Directory* for North West Surrey lists shops and businesses in the High Street. They include: F.W. Beetham, outfitter's; E.W. Elliott, carpenter; E. Cocks, printer; J. Clarkson, picture framer; H.P. Bassett, photographer; Home and Colonial Stores; T. Pursell, hairdresser; F. Wyatt, gents' and ladies' outfitter's; Seaman & Son, butcher's; Locke & Son, grocer's; A. Brown, oil and colour merchant's; E.N. Farrow, cycle maker's; Mrs. J.M. Ecroyd, confectioner's; and C.F. Williams, draper's.

The shops in The Quadrant area were erected in 1897, the year of Queen Victoria's Diamond Jubilee. This area had been part of the Portmore Park estate, purchased by the Locke King family and sold off for redevelopment from the 1880s. One firm operating here was Lewis & Sons. The business was originally started in 1884 by Mr. Walter Levermore, who opened a shop in South Road and later the High Street, selling cycle frames, and bicycles made by Humber, Rover, Swift and Singer. Sewing machines were also sold and bicycles repaired. Around 1907 the business was called The Holstein Cycle Works. Another shop was opened in 1908 in Limes Parade in The Quadrant, and shortly after Mr. W.L. Lewis was taken on as manager; he later married Mr. Levermore's daughter. In the years leading up to the First World War the business thrived and by the 1920s it was known as the Heath Road Branch of Levermore's. In the 1930s the premises were enlarged to accommodate more showroom space, and B.S.A. motor bikes were sold along with Triumphs and Nortons. Mr. W.L. Lewis inherited the business, and on his death in 1954 it passed to his two sons. By this

time it specialised in motor bikes. After the British motor cycle trade collapsed in the late 1960s because of strong Japanese competition, the shop remained one of the few stockists left selling B.S.A spare parts, which in the 1970s and '80s were sent all over the world. The premises closed in 1987 on the retirement of the Lewis brothers.

Luxford's was a family removal firm which opened a warehouse in The Quadrant in 1926. In 1908 Luxford's had run a fruit shop here and later they sold babies' and children's clothes.

Off The Quadrant was a large timber-framed house called 'The Limes', which was once the property of Mrs. Maceroni, widow of Colonel Francis Maceroni, aide-de-camp to Murat, King of Naples. Mrs. Maceroni took in many lodgers at 'The Limes', including the novelist and poet George Meredith (1828-1909), who lived there with his wife during the first years of their marriage.

When travelling from Windsor Castle to visit her son and daughter-in-law, the Duke and Duchess of Albany at Claremont in Esher, Queen Victoria used the winding lane known as Grange Road. Grange Road was known as Common Road at its Hersham end because of the link with Burwood Park. The area of common land preserved for public use at the end of Queen's Road was used originally for gravel extraction and as a result a small pond developed, known as The Green. The pond was filled in after the

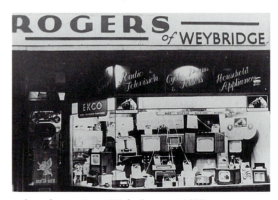

72   View of W. Levermore, manufacturer and cycle repairer, High Street, c.1930.

73   The front window of Rogers of Weybridge, 51 High Street, 1950s. This interesting view shows a selection of the latest television sets available, along with the radios made famous by Rogers.

74 View of the shops in The Quadrant, *c*.1910. Luxford's removal firm can be seen across the street with the spire of St James's Church rising in the distance.

First World War, although a shallow depression can still be seen in the ground.

The road has been dominated by large houses for many years. One such house, Brackley Lodge, was built on land between Queen's Road and the London and South Western Railway. At one time the area was part of Oatlands estate but Lord Egerton owned the estate in 1844. Brackley Lodge was developed between 1964-7 into a residential estate and after the original house was demolished the grounds were divided up into building plots.

Other notable houses in the area have been Manby Lodge on the western side of Queen's Road, with grounds adjoining The Common and the railway station. It consisted of three reception rooms, six bedrooms and a bathroom and was offered on a 99-year lease from 1897 by a Miss Wright. A house called The Hollies (formerly Westernhay) was demolished in 1997 and the site used for more residential development. Many other large houses were built in the locality in the 1920s and '30s, particularly off High Pines Close. From the 1860s the area saw much residential development for the mid-

dle classes. The Conservative Land Society developed property off Queen's Road in a development called The Weybridge Estate. Up until 1868 only property owners had the right to vote and the 'Conservative Land Society' had been set up in 1852, after the Tory Party lost the general election, to build houses and to provide the middle classes with a vote—which they hoped would be for them.

A site comprising three roods and four perches was bought in a triangle of land bordered by Queen's Road and the railway line and purchasers paid £50 to acquire shares in the Society. By 1857 the Society had 22 estates nationwide. The Weybridge Estate was developed from the mid-1860s offering houses from £400 (exclusive of stables) to £700 for two semi-detached properties. Plots 71-4 were purchased by Mr. Benjamin Scott to build the new Congregational Church, now the United Reformed Church. After 1868 owning property was no longer a requirement for voting and the need for the politically linked Land Societies disappeared. The Conservative Land Society was liquidated in 1890 and the Liberal Freehold Land

75   Temple Market, on the corner of Queens Road and Oatlands Drive, *c.*1930-2.

Society was absorbed into the Abbey Building Society.

From the 1920s the mainly residential Queen's Road became a thriving commercial area. One well-known shop until 1971 was Melbourn's Fishmonger's, run by Frank Melbourn from 1936. He joined the army during the First World War at 15 years of age and in the 1920s went to work at Billingsgate Fish Market in London. He managed John Eighteen's Fishmonger's in Queen's Road from 1936 until 1959, when he bought the business. He remembered selling kippers at 1½d. for two and 2d. for five fish. He never had a holiday in his life and retired in 1971. Many of his customers had shopped with him since the 1930s. Other notable businesses in Queen's Road in the mid-1970s were the Walters Family Butcher's, who have had a business in Weybridge since 1817. Edmeds supplied uniforms to the British Army during the Great War, and Cave Brothers established a cabinet-making business in 1918. There was also an Odeon Cinema in Queen's Street which opened in 1934 but closed

in 1960. It was used as a Catholic church until it was demolished in the late 1980s.

The last major retail development in Weybridge was Temple Market shopping parade. This was built on land at the top of Monument Hill, facing the Cricket Green Common, near the War Memorial. It was started in 1930 by Horace Thompson of Hersham and was built as a single-storey shopping parade, with lock-up stalls for the storage of sales counters and produce. Mr. Thompson owned land opposite Hersham railway station, from where he ran a nursery. By 1932 the premises were expanded to include 10 shops with flats above. They were built in a typical 1930s style of low lines, white-washed walls and ridged green glazed pantiles. When someone enquired of Mr. Thompson whether he was building a market or a temple he was so amused that he named the new development Temple Market. Mrs. Grundy had a tea shop on the premises which sold Art Deco novelties and decorations from 1935 until the Second World War.

Twelve

A Place to Worship

The Elmbridge area contains one of the oldest churches in Surrey, St Mary's at Stoke D'Abernon near Cobham, whose origins go back to the Anglo-Saxon period. There is also evidence that those parts of the church dating back to the Anglo-Saxon period used stone from Roman buildings. However, for the purpose of this chapter we are examining the churches built in Weybridge since the Middle Ages.

Church of St Nicholas

The Domesday Survey of 1086 does not mention a church in Weybridge, although a chapel was built later that was attached firstly to Chertsey Abbey and later Newark Priory.

The first church was a small medieval building that survived until 1849, when it was replaced by the present building. With the opening of the London to Southampton railway in 1838 and the influx of population, the small medieval church became inadequate. The necessary funds were raised and the church was built by J.L. Pearson, who later designed Truro Cathedral, in the fashionable Gothic Revival style of the time. The church steeple is 150 ft. high and can be seen for miles. The new church was enlarged in 1864 to cater for the ever-expanding population of the area.

Brayley describes the older church thus:

Weybridge Church was dedicated to St James, or, according to Ecton, to St Nicholas, as it now stands in the Ecclesiastical Register. It consists of a nave, a small chapel, and a south aisle; but has undergone so many alterations that no vestige of the original structure is discoverable. At the west end is a modern entrance porch decorated in front by pilasters supporting an entablature, with triglyphs. A small wooden tower, crowned by a shingled spire, rises from the gable of the roof, and contains three bells and a clock. The nave is separated from the south side by angular columns, fluted, which support a large gallery extending the whole length of that side: this gallery was built by subscription, and the seats are all private property. An inscription states that 'these columns were erected, A.D. 1722'. In the gallery that crosses the west end of the nave is a small organ, which was presented to the church by Mr. Worthington, of Orchard-house, who likewise defrayed the expense of altering the gallery. About four hundred and fifty persons are accommodated in this edifice: the pews are painted white, and regularly numbered.

76   Print of St Nicholas Church by Cracklow, 1823.

77 The chancel at Weybridge Parish Church, showing the East Wall which was printed with life-size figures of Moses and Elias and a purple curtain drawn up revealing cherubim and clouds. Admiral Hopson's memorial is on the North Wall. The gallery was added in 1720. The painting is a copy made by Miss D. Grenside of an original in the collection at the British Museum, dated 1822.

78 Pen and ink drawing of the proposed new church and the old church (on the same scale) of St Nicholas, *c*.1846-7. This was obviously used to show the great improvement that would be brought when the new church was built.

Brayley gives special attention to the memorial erected in honour of Frederica Charlotte Ulrica, the late wife of the Duke of York, who died in Weybridge in 1820. He writes that:

> The pews in the south gallery are neatly lined and many are carpeted. That which was occupied by the late duke and duchess of York, and which belongs to the Oatlands estate, is very handsomely fitted up, and furnished with chairs. Over the entrance to this part of the gallery, at the east end, is the beautiful mural monument to the DUCHESS OF YORK, which was executed by Chantrey in the year 1823, and may be closely ranked with his elegant Memorial of the Children in Lichfield Cathedral, both for design and execution. The duchess is represented by an alto-relievo, the size of life. She appears clad in a Grecian robe, loosely fastened by a brooch at the shoulder; the arms being uncovered, and the hair confined by a tiara. The position is devotional; the hands are crossed over the breast; and the sight directed upwards towards a celestial crown of stars.

Monuments from the church of St Nicholas were transferred to the new St James's when it opened in 1848, including three skeleton brasses dating from the 1400s. Other brasses transferred from the old church include those of local people, John Woulde (1598), Thomas Inwood (1586) and Sir John Trevor (1605). After the opening of the new church in 1848 the old one became redundant and was subsequently demolished in 1849.

St James's Church, 1848

The Rev. J.E. Tarbat wrote a book in 1898 entitled *Some Account of the Ecclesiastical History of Weybridge*, in which he described the circumstances that led to building a new church for the village as follows:

> By the middle of the present century the old church was found to be far too small for the population. It was accordingly decided, not without some opposition, to pull down the existing structure and to erect a new and more commodious church to the south of the original building on a portion of the glebe land given by the Rector, the Rev. William Giffard. The new church, designed by the late Mr. Pearson,

capable of holding 608 persons, was constructed in 1848, being dedicated to St James. The old church is said to have been dedicated to St Nicholas, but there is some doubt as to that being the case. At any rate Willis, in his *Survey of Cathedrals*, published in 1729, speaks of the parish church as 'St James'.

Thomas Feetham promoted the idea for a new church, together with Dr. Spyers (who ran a school for young gentlemen at Holstein House, High Street). They persuaded the rector, the Rev. William Giffard, to join them in fundraising for the new building. However, the idea of demolishing the old church caused division in the village, and upset many of the older villagers who had relatives buried in the churchyard. A number of verses were written to express opposition to the new building:

> Oh, spare our sacred village pile,
> Nor raise it to the ground;
> Our parents rest beneath its aisle,
> Our children in its ground.

79 St James's Church, by Walmsley, *c*.1848. On the back of the print is written 'Consecration of St James's Church, Weybridge. On Saturday June 17th, 1848. The service to commence at Eleven. The Clergy are requested to attend in their robes.'

80 *Left*. Interior view of St James's Church painted in 1867. This shows the church in almost its original condition as built in 1848. Since it was painted, many alterations have been made to the interior.

81 *Below left*. Portrait of Edward Rose, rector of Weybridge from 1855-82, drawn by William Fyfe in 1856.

82 *Below right*. The Rev. W.B. Money, rector of St James's Church after the death of the Rev. Rose.

Many of the villagers apparently rushed to the demolition site and rescued many objects, such as a Jacobean candelabra and a clock later sold into private hands. Many family memorials were also saved and later reinstated in the new church. The altar was in private hands until it was used in the cemetery chapel in Brooklands Lane and is now the nave altar at St James's. A large section of plaster showing cherubim with clouds and a curtain was rescued and is now at Elmbridge Museum. The old church bells were brought to the new church, but were melted down in 1875 when new bells were cast.

The new church was consecrated on 17 June 1848 by the Bishop of Winchester and the Rev. William Giffard. He died in 1855 of tuberculosis and was replaced by the Rev. Edward Rose, who in 1865 started the *Parish Magazine*. A war shrine was opened in 1917 and in 1919 the south chapel was dedicated to the war dead, becoming the Chapel of All Souls.

Edward Rose died in 1883 and was buried in the churchyard. A collection in his memory raised nearly £500 and a window was placed in his honour in the south-west corner of the church depicting the life of Jesus and scenes from the pastoral life of a priest. The Rev. Walter Money then took over the running of the church. The Rev. Spence Buller was rector of St James's for the first part of the century, having taken up the position in 1903. He eventually resigned in 1923 due to poor health.

Over the years many alterations have been made to the church: in 1856 a 150-ft. high spire was added, a small chapel was built in 1858, and a south chapel added in 1865. New bells were installed in 1874, a marble pavement was laid in 1883, and in 1885 the chancel arch was raised and lengthened by 10 feet, new steps were built and the east window was rebuilt. Also, a reredos of red and white Derbyshire alabaster was erected in the church, and in 1893 more alabaster was applied to the walls of the chancel and mosaics laid.

In 1897 the St Alban's Mission Hall was opened at the junction of Portmore Park Road and St Alban's Avenue. In 1908 the Parish Room was opened on land facing onto Church Street.

St Michael's Church

By 1865 there were 1,000 people attending St James's on a regular basis and in 1872 it was decided another church was needed. This was called St Michael's and was built in Prince's Road to a design by architect William Butterfield. It was consecrated in 1874, on St James's Day, by the Bishop of Winchester.

The church was finally closed in 1973 because of declining membership, and the remaining congregation transferred to St James's Church.

St Charles Borromeo Church

In 1734 Philip Southcote, a Catholic, purchased Woburn Park Estate, Chertsey, where he established a Roman Catholic mission. Masses were held in the family home, 'Nutfield'. By 1815 the estate had passed out of Catholic hands and the priest in charge, Father Peter Potier, who had been in charge of the estate, moved to Weybridge where he continued the mission until 1834.

In 1835 James Taylor built a small family chapel on his own land facing the Heath. At the time Weybridge had only a small Catholic community. A religious census taken on 30 March 1851 showed that only 50 people used the Catholic chapel of St Charles Borromeo. Only ever intended for family worship, it became internationally famous after February 1848, when the French King, Louis Philippe, abdicated and took up residence at Claremont, Esher. Claremont was Crown property and not suitable for Catholic worship, so on 7 March 1848 the King and Queen attended mass at James Taylor's small chapel. Thus began the connection with the royal family of Orleans, 13 of whose members were buried in the vault beneath the chapel. The bodies were later removed to Dreux, France, to be interred alongside family members. The last interment was of ex-King Manoel of Portugal, in 1932. The last body to be removed to Dreux was that of the Duchess of Nemours, cousin to Queen Victoria, in 1979.

The original chapel was built in a Byzantine design, but a much larger church was built on the site in 1882. The church has

83   St Michael's Church, Princes Road, shortly before it was demolished in 1973.

84 & 85   Two views of the Roman Catholic Church of St Charles Borromeo. The bottom left picture shows the church from the front in Heath Road, *c.*1907-10, and the bottom right illustration, the rear view, *c.*1930.

had a chequered history in the last few years. It was closed and its congregation moved to a new church in Minorca Fields. In 1988 an application was made for its demolition and replacement by flats. This led to a public outcry and a campaign to save the building was launched. It was eventually sold to a Korean Church who now safeguard its future.

Weybridge Congregational Church

Weybridge has had a history of nonconformity since the 1680s. During the reign of Charles II, Archbishop Sheldon reported that there was a 'conventicle at Weybridge, at the house of John Tilley; teacher, Mr. James'. Later, in 1855 the Rev. A.E. Lord of Hersham was accused of preaching in a cottage in Thames Street.

In 1860 Benjamin Scott, Chamberlain of the City of London, came to live at Heath House, now called Lorimar House, on the edge of the Common. Mr. Scott frequently walked to church in Hersham and later organised joint open-air services in Weybridge between the Baptist, Congregational and Wesleyan ministers. A billiard room at Fir Grove was set aside for indoor meetings. The arrangement lasted until 1862 when it was decided something permanent should be organised. Benjamin Scott approached the rector of St James's Church to see if they could share evening services. Not surprisingly, the rector, Edward Rose, declined. Not to be defeated, Scott used his newly built music room at Heath House to conduct services, holding his first meeting in 1863. As numbers increased, Scott built a lecture hall in his grounds. He invited his friend, Mr. Baron, down to Weybridge to help run the services, and Mr. Baron moved to a house in Prince's Road in 1864. A decision was then taken to build a church.

Plans for a permanent building proceeded apace and land was purchased from the Conservative Land Society in Queen's Road. Subscriptions were taken out to help pay for the construction of a Congregational Church and building began in July 1864. The builder was Frank Saunders of London and the architect was John Tarring, who designed the new church in

86 Print of the proposed Congregational Church, Queen's Road, taken from the diaries of the Rev. Baron.

87 The Rev. Baron, minister of the Congregational Church from 1865-80.

Gothic style. Disaster struck during the building on 5 November 1864, as recorded by the *Surrey Comet*:

> For some time past a splendid edifice intended for a Congregational Church has been in course of erection on Weybridge Common opposite York Road and was approaching completion. Just after breakfast time on Saturday morning [28 October 1864], as men were getting to their places in various parts of the building, especially on the tower which is about 80 feet high and where some men were putting on ornamental tiles, the whole structure gave way, the side walls that took the broad span of the roof bulged out and the tower toppled over, the whole coming to the ground with a fearful crash.

Thankfully nobody was killed. Rebuilding soon began and the total cost came to £2,100. In 1865 the Weybridge Congregational Church was formally constituted and Mr. Baron became its first minister, and was employed on £60 a year; Benjamin Scott became deacon. The dedication of the building took place on 17 May, and afterwards the workmen and their wives were invited to tea at Mr. Scott's house. Building work continued on the Sunday School premises. In 1866 Mr. Baron was ordained and received a stipend of £120 per annum, by which time a lecture hall had been built for the church. Three years later, Rev. Baron received an increased stipend and a gold watch from his congregation. In 1870 a day school was established at the church, to provide an alternative to the National School run by St James's Church, which was run on Anglican lines.

In the 1880s extra work was carried out in the church, which included enlarging the Sunday School accommodation, repainting the interior, building an extra transept, strengthening the ceiling and adding a gallery. In 1890 Rev. Baron resigned after 25 years' service at the church, and went to live in Hastings, dying in Mortlake in 1899. The church celebrated its centenary in 1965. During 1997-8 the church exterior was totally cleaned and repaired, revealing the lovely colour of the stone-work, which had been hidden for many years beneath layers of grime.

88   The Rev. Baron's Sunday School teachers, *c.*1870.

Weybridge Methodist Church

Methodism began in Weybridge in the late 1890s when Mr. and Mrs. F.W. Beetham invited their neighbours to attend a service at their home. By 1900 there were enough people attending to justify a decision to build a church. Land was given to the trustees of the project by Mr. Wood of Walton-on-Thames, who had purchased it for £500. In early 1900 the trustees appointed Mr. Gunton, a London architect, to design the building and Mr. W. Greenfield was given a contract for £2,750 to build the church. The foundation stone was laid on 2 June 1900. By 1920 the trustees had repaid all their debts and the church was theirs. The first pastor was the Rev. W.H. Tindall, who came to live in the district. In 1937 the Hayfield Hall was built on land adjoining the church and used for the Sunday School and social functions. During the Second World War, the women of the church ran a canteen from the hall for soldiers stationed in the area. It ran three nights a week from 1940-6; entertainment included table-tennis, chess and draughts. In 1977 the building caught fire, though fortunately most of the damage was caused by the smoke. Repairs were carried out and the church re-opened on 14 September 1980. In the interim, the congregation met in the undamaged Hayfield Hall.

St Martin De Pores

St Martin De Pores was a Catholic church located in the old Odeon Cinema in Queen's Road Weybridge. It opened in 1964, four years after the cinema had closed. The church remained in the building until the late 1980s when it was demolished and modern shops built on the site.

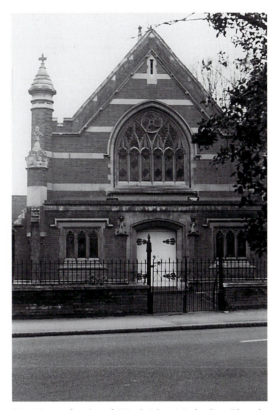

89 Front façade of Weybridge Methodist Church, c.1988.

Since the Second World War the religious atmosphere of Weybridge has become both multicultural and multi-faith, with Jews, Hindus and Muslims, as well as others, living and worshipping in the locality. The facilities created for these groups are too diverse to list here; the overall intention of this chapter has been to concentrate on the religious *heritage* of the village, which is predominantly a Christian one.

Thirteen

Public Service

Before the creation of modern local government in the late 19th century, local affairs were based on the existing civil parishes. Weybridge Vestry maintained the roads and provided for the parish poor through the Poor Relief. The nearby Walton-on-Thames Vestry also employed local police constables until the creation of the Surrey Police Force in 1850.

From the 1840s Parliament was concerned about the standards of public health, and wished to minimise the risk of cholera and other infectious diseases. As a result, new bodies were established to maintain public health. The Chertsey Board of Guardians of the Poor were responsible for the administration of Poor Relief in Walton-on-Thames and the Weybridge area

until it was replaced by the Chertsey Rural Sanitary Authority in 1872. In the 1860s drainage committees were established to organise the laying of efficient and sanitary drainage to the new houses and businesses in the area. Highways boards were also established in the 1860s to maintain the roads in the different parishes. Burial boards were founded in the 1870s to raise the necessary funds to purchase the land to build and maintain cemeteries. At the same time, lighting inspectors were appointed for the provision of adequate street lighting. School boards were also appointed in the late 1870s to take over the running of schools that failed to meet government regulations outlined in the 1870 Education Act.

90 Weybridge Urban District Council refuse cart decorated for May Day, *c.*1905.

The Urban District Council

Parliament's first attempt at rationalising local administration was in 1889, when it established county councils. In 1895 it replaced the whole local government structure of separate boards and committees with ratepayer-elected urban district councils, the beginning of modern local government. The proposal to create a separate council for Weybridge was first mooted by the Weybridge Vestry, who successfully petitioned Surrey County Council to have its own district council. Surrey County Council allocated 12 members to the new Weybridge Urban District Council. Elections were held in December 1894 and the Council had its first meeting in a classroom at the National School in Baker Street on 2 January 1895; Mr. Till was elected the first chairman. District councils were also established at Walton-on-Thames, Esher and the Dittons, as well as East and West Molesey.

The new councillors sat on various committees which oversaw the provision of services paid for out of the rates. These included provision (or regulation) of allotments, cemeteries, drainage, fire brigades, gas and electricity supplies, hospitals, housing, libraries, public halls, museums, parks and sports and recreation grounds, road maintenance, refuse collection, schools, street lighting and water supply. In the early years the local rates hardly varied from one year to the next. In 1896 the rate was 4s. 5d. compared with 4s. 6d. in 1918. However, the rate collected for Poor Relief did increase from 1s. 7d. in 1896 to 3s. 8d. in 1918.

The lasting effects of the First World War were varied. The Council found that local rate-payers expected provision of more public services than before the war. This included more modern housing for the poor, better maintenance of the public highways, plus the provision of leisure and recreational facilities. The Local Government Act of 1929 proposed merging the smaller urban and rural district councils to form larger administrative units. At this time Weybridge had a population of 6,702 and a rateable value of £98,744. In 1932 the Walton and Weybridge councils were merged together, and the first joint council meeting was held on 28 March 1933 at the Elmgrove council offices in Walton-on-Thames. Mr. Saunders was chairman and Mr. Froude vice-chairman; both were councillors at Walton-on-Thames, and Weybridge had a minority position on the council.

In 1933 the building of a new road in Walton-on-Thames, which would be called New Zealand Avenue, began. In 1935 the Burvale burial ground was purchased. By 1938 the worsening political situation with Germany required the Walton and Weybridge Urban District Council to implement preparations against air raids, and the first civil defence workers were employed; the council also purchased 30,000 gas masks and sandbags to protect buildings from bomb blast.

During the war the district suffered its fair share of bomb damage. When peace was declared it was suffering from a major housing shortage. Plans were put into action to build council houses and by 1954 1,000 had been built, but there was still a large waiting list so a points scheme was adopted to rationalise the system. Other developments included the building of a public hall in Weybridge from 1956 and the construction of a library and museum building in Church Street (in partnership with Surrey County Council) which finally opened in 1967. In 1966 a new Town Hall in Walton-on-Thames was opened by Princess Margaret and a year earlier a brand new swimming pool and leisure complex was opened in Walton as well.

In 1972 Parliament again reorganised local government in England and Wales by merging the former urban districts into borough councils. Walton and Weybridge and Esher Urban District Councils were merged to form Elmbridge Borough Council from April 1974; the county council structure was retained. The new authority covered 23,895 acres, and with a population of 116,480 people, the rateable value was £20 million. In 1994-5 another piecemeal reorganisation of local government was intended to replace the two-tier structure with unitary authorities; however, Surrey retained the two-tier structure created in 1974.

91   The junction of Baker Street and the High Street, with Aberdeen House on the right, *c.*1910. Aberdeen House was the offices for the Weybridge Urban District Council.

Weybridge Town Hall

Weybridge U.D.C. first met at the National School in Baker Street in January 1895, but these were inadequate premises and the authority later leased a house in Baker Street for £40 a year. In 1908 Aberdeen House, on the corner of Baker Street and High Street, was purchased for £4,500 which included the house itself, together with a shop, stables and some land. This remained the property of the Council until 1933 when the offices were moved to Elmgrove, though Aberdeen House continued to be used by the medical officer until 1966 and the public museum until 1967. It was finally leased to Lloyds Bank who demolished the house and built a bank on the site.

Allotments

The Council administered some allotments on land just off Churchfields, at the rear of St James's Church. In 1800, 72 acres of common land were made over to poor cottagers. This formed the area known as The Heath and the Cricket Green. The 1882 Allotments Extension Act proposed to enclose six acres for allotments. To prevent this happening, the Heath Preservation Society was formed to stop the heathland being cultivated.

The Society leased 10 acres for 30 years at £50 a year, and the allotments went to Churchfields instead. Originally those lands formed as a result of enclosure were administered by trustees, but this duty passed to the Council in 1934.

Drainage

The major reason for creating proper local government was originally the supervision of public health. Until the 1860s the management of sewage and waste disposal was inadequate. Weybridge's sewage was drained into cesspits and ditches, usually contaminating local soil and rivers. In 1867 the Government banned this practice, and the Weybridge Vestry was forced to apply for funding to help finance the installation of a sewer. The old Weybridge sewer had consisted of a drain running from the High Street to Thames Street which discharged the sewage into the Broadwater. Naturally this was a source of great complaint to the Vestry, but nothing was really done until the Council was created in 1895. A sewer pipe was laid from Oatlands to Thames Street and then to a collection tank in Walton Lane; the effluent was then pumped into a works newly built at New Haw. Another drain was laid in 1910 at the southern end of the authority near Byfleet Road. In 1973 the New Haw plant was completely rebuilt.

Rainwater was simply collected in ditches running along the side of the road, until they required pumping out. The greatest recorded rainfall in the area was during September 1968 when 3.23 inches of rain fell over a period of 7½ hours causing the River Mole to burst its banks and flood many of the towns and villages in the area. Afterwards, £2 million was spent on flood alleviation work.

Electricity

The Weybridge Electricity Supply Company was given a Provisional Lighting Order in 1891 and built a power generating station in Church Walk. Soon electric street lighting was illuminating the gloom of Weybridge. However, there was much local opposition to the new-fangled electric lights, partly because the power was supplied over ground on unsightly wooden poles which many thought ugly and obtrusive. The Council decided against the new system and declined to renew the contract for the lighting of its streets with electricity, trusting instead to the cheaper gas lighting. It was not until 1900 that the Urban

Electricity Supply Company secured a lighting order for Weybridge. At Easter 1902 a new generating works was completed in Thames Street, but the plant closed in 1922 after power was acquired from elsewhere. In 1932 the Urban Electricity Supply Company was merged with the Home Counties Joint Electricity Authority, which in turn was integrated into the National Grid.

The Fire Brigade

Long before the creation of the District Council, Weybridge had a volunteer fire brigade. This was the brainchild of John William Young, at one time a master builder in the employ of the Hon. Peter Locke King. In 1874 he appealed for volunteer recruits and secured the use of an old manual pump. A year later a committee was formed and the Hon. Hugh Locke King was elected the first Captain of the Brigade, an honorary post. The brigade attended their first fire at the Weybridge Oil Mills at Whittet's Ait on 24 December 1877, when the mill was engulfed in a major conflagration.

The brigade was totally reliant on voluntary donations to purchase the necessary equipment, including a Merryweather manual fire engine, and to fund its activities. In 1879 it was reorganised

92 The Weybridge Electricity Works, *c.*1905.

93 Members of the Weybridge Fire Brigade shortly after attending a fire at Whittet's Mill in 1878.

94 Weybridge Fire Brigade seen here on their Merryweather fire engine in 1916. The photograph was taken by Mr. J. Cecil Gould.

and Thomas Dix became its captain; a well-known figure in the village, he was also a master butcher. He used his own horses to draw the engine. In 1881 the brigade moved into new accommodation in Balfour Road after land was granted to it by Hugh Locke King.

With the creation of the District Council in 1895 the fortunes of the brigade improved. A council committee was set up which took over responsibility for the operation and funding of the brigade—though it was still run on a voluntary basis with no paid employees. In 1902 the council decided to purchase a steam pump to replace the manual pump which had required

over thirty men to operate it (and copious amounts of beer to keep them happy). As a result, a Merryweather steam pump was purchased, and shortly after that an electric alarm bell system was installed at key locations in the village to alert members of the brigade in the event of a fire. This system was supplied and maintained by the National Telephone Company. In June 1907 the founder, John Young, died aged 69 years. He was conducted to his funeral service at the Weybridge Congregational Church on a fire engine bedecked with flowers, with 150 firemen in attendance.

John Walter Brooker, the proprietor of a laundry business in Thames Street, Weybridge, was elected the new chief officer in 1907. In 1908 the brigade attended two fires and three false alarms. The following year it was called out several times to douse fires on Weybridge Heath, sometimes started deliberately by boys. In 1909 the brigade had a hooter installed at the Electricity Light Works to warn them of any fire in the district.

Later chief officers included A. Hasslacher, who was in the post between 1908-13, and Mr. Horsell. In 1914 the brigade acquired a Merryweather petrol-driven fire tender for £720—this was a 'Light Brigade' model Hatfield Motor Fire Engine, capable of pumping 200-250 gallons a minute. Two years later Mr. Wood became chief officer. In 1920 the brigade attended a fire at St George's Hill golf clubhouse, which was totally gutted because the brigade were unable to obtain the right water pressure on the hill. Martynside Aircraft Works also had a serious fire in September 1920. In 1924 Chief Officer Wood died and was also carried to his funeral on the Weybridge fire engine decorated with flowers.

With the union of the Walton and Weybridge Councils in 1933, the brigade was merged with that of Walton-on-Thames. In 1941 the brigade was merged into the National Fire Service, and in 1947 all the independent fire brigades in Surrey came under the control of Surrey County Council.

Gas Supply

The Walton and Weybridge Gas Company was formed in 1869 and established a gas and coke plant, with a gas-holder, in Manor Road, Walton-on-Thames. Weybridge Vestry appointed a Lighting Board to regulate the supply and their powers were passed over to the Weybridge Urban District Council in 1895. Gas lighting continued in use until 1932. The Walton and Weybridge Gas Company was nationalised in 1949 and soon afterwards the Walton plant was closed down and dismantled.

Hospitals

Weybridge acquired its first hospital in 1889 when the Weybridge Cottage Hospital was opened in what was to become the Locke King Clinic in Balfour Road. This was a hospital run by volunteers and maintained by public subscription; its purpose was to provide an alternative to the workhouse infirmary then available to the poor (from 1837 all paupers from Walton and Weybridge had been transferred to the Union Workhouse at Chertsey, where parishioners too poor to pay for their own medical treatment were seen). The workhouse system continued until 1928-9 when the Poor Law was repealed and the workhouse infirmary put under the control of Surrey County Council. From 1895 all outbreaks of infectious disease had to be

95 Weybridge Cottage Hospital in Balfour Road in the 1920s.

reported to the chief medical officer of Weybridge Council. The hospital was expanded in 1908 when the parish room, located next to the hospital, was converted into a women's ward. This was paid for by Mrs. Rooke. By 1923 it was evident that a new hospital was required and a fund-raising campaign was started with appeals through the British Red Cross. Hugh Locke King solved the problem of land for the hospital site by donating Vigo House in Church Street. The hospital was opened in January 1928. There had been a clinic in Vigo House prior to the rebuilding, and this was transferred to the new hospital, now renamed the Locke King Clinic after Dame Ethel Locke King, who had funded it.

Council Housing

From its inception Weybridge U.D.C. was concerned with local housing needs and the regulation of properties. Inspectors regularly visited dwellings in the neighbourhood. The Working Classes Act of 1890 allowed councils to build rate-subsidised homes for the working classes. Weybridge U.D.C. officers inspected houses in the new Letchworth Garden City and admired the environment, although they criticised the quality of the buildings. A housing shortage existed after the First World War and a new Act of Parliament induced local authorities to build more. The Council started to build the Old Palace Gardens estate from 1923, consisting of 160 houses which were not completed until 1927, at an average cost of £370-£450 each. When the Government stopped subsidising the building of council houses in 1933, the Council had constructed 169.

In May 1945 Walton and Weybridge Council found themselves with a housing crisis, as there had been no domestic building during the war and many houses in the district had been totally destroyed or badly damaged. The council adopted a points system for the allocation of existing houses to those in greatest need, and a council house building scheme was quickly put into place. This scheme was so successful that by 1954 the Council had built 1,000 houses in the area.

Library and Museum

A Libraries Act of 1893 gave local authorities the powers to fund their own libraries from the rates, although by 1865 the village already had a library of sorts because the rector of St James's had started one up in his house. In November 1884 a subscription library was established in the parish room in Balfour Road; this opened twice a week and cost one penny a month. Weybridge's first public library was established in the Weybridge Church Hall in 1924 with help from Surrey County Council. When Walton and Weybridge Councils merged the library moved to the first floor of the former council offices in Aberdeen House.

In 1874 an Exhibition of Art, Industries and Manufactures was held under the aegis of the Weybridge Mutual Improvement Society and Literary Institute in their hall in Church Street. The hall had been presented to the Society by Peter J. Locke King in 1873. It is now the Conservative Club. In 1906 a seventh exhibition was held in Holstein Hall and was well attended. The *Surrey Times* reported that they hoped the exhibition could be repeated and perhaps made into a permanent museum. When the Council purchased Aberdeen House in 1908 from the butcher, Washington Dale, the *Surrey Advertiser* proposed that a museum be established there

> with a view to retaining for the town the many item of local interest which would otherwise be lost. There are many people in Weybridge who have relics going back several hundred years; and any such objects which were presented to the museum the Council would take due care of and hand on to the future generations.

A committee was formed in February 1909 that aimed to raise the necessary funds to equip a museum room in the new council building, and the following appeal was issued:

> It has been resolved to establish a Museum at Weybridge for the preservation of local antiquities and objects illustrating the geology, fauna, and flora of the neighbourhood, together with such books on these subjects as would be useful for reference, and it is

96 The Weybridge Mutual Improvement Society and Literary Institute, seen here shortly after it was opened in 1873.

believed that such a collection will have distinctly educational value for all classes. In the new offices the Council has granted the use of a commodious room, on the distinct condition that the cost of supplying cases and bookshelves be defrayed by voluntary subscription. After the initial outlay, nothing will be needed but the donation, or loan, of such interesting objects of the kind referred to as residents and friends may be willing to contribute. In order that the Urban District Council may become the legal custodians of the fittings and contents, it is proposed to adopt 'The Museums Act, 1891'.

Dr. Eric Gardner, a local G.P., was appointed honorary curator of the museum, with Miss Harting as his assistant. The original museum committee was strengthened by the addition of Mr. P. Pilditch, Mr. W. Reed, Mr. J. Brooker and Mrs. Percy Leake. On the Council Mr. George Chambers and Dr. Henry Willson were very supportive of the scheme. The Weybridge Museum was opened to the public on 23 June 1909 by Sir Charles Holroyd, director of the National Gallery, who lived at Sturdie House, Oatlands Park.

In 1915 the Council met the costs of stationery, stamps, printing of posters, and new furniture and fittings when necessary. Staff were still unpaid, although they were regularly giving lectures. Miss Dorothy Grenside was appointed hon. assistant curator and compiled a hand-

printed catalogue of the museum collections to date. In 1933 the museum came under the control of the new local authority and started to collect items relating to the area covered by Walton-on-Thames and the surrounding villages. During the Second World War the museum was closed and all the exhibits packed away for safe keeping. Dr. Gardner fell ill in the summer of 1947 and responsibility for the museum fell to Miss Grenside. She organised the move of the museum back into Aberdeen House, this time to a room on the first floor because the library downstairs had expanded. Dr. Watts reopened the museum on 17 September 1948 and 50-60 people attended.

Dr. Gardner died in 1951, and the title of honorary curator passed to Miss Grenside. In 1963 she retired and the Council decided to rehouse the museum in a new library building being planned by Surrey County Council. Two permanent fully paid members of staff were appointed, curator Mr. Brian Blake and later his assistant, Mrs. Avril Lansdell, and the service moved to new premises on the first floor of the museum and library building in Church Street. Avril Lansdell became curator when Brian Blake left to work elsewhere, and remained in the post until she took early retirement in late 1989. By this time, the collection had expanded dramatically to cover all aspects of the history of the area from prehistoric times, as well as its

natural history and geology. From 1974 the Weybridge Museum became the local authority museum service for the 17 towns and villages covered by Elmbridge Borough Council. From 1984 several staff helped establish a museum at Brooklands to record its unique aviation and motor-racing history. Elmbridge Borough Council funded the establishment of a Brooklands Museum, which eventually became an independent trust.

In 1991 the museum was renamed Elmbridge Museum to reflect its new role. In 1994 it successfully applied for a grant from the Heritage Lottery Fund to help pay for the cost of refurbishing the exhibition gallery. From November 1995 the museum closed for refurbishment and was re-opened on 10 December 1996.

Water Supply

In 1869 the West Surrey Water Company was formed to pipe water to Weybridge as well as the neighbouring towns of Walton-on-Thames, Chertsey, Byfleet and Shepperton. The water was taken from the Thames at Walton and filtered then pumped to storage reservoirs on St George's Hill from where it was distributed by gravity to Walton-on-Thames and Weybridge. By 1901 most houses in Weybridge had access to running water. In 1960 the company became part of the Woking and District Water Company. The district contains a number of important reservoirs mostly situated around Walton-on-Thames and Molesey; these include the Apps Court Reservoir (1875 and 1896), Sunbury Reservoir (1911), and, more recently, the Queen Elizabeth II Reservoir (1962).

The Post Office

Weybridge Post Office was originally in Heath Road, but by the early 1900s this was having difficulty coping with the demands made on it by the ever-increasing population. Plans were laid to replace it with a new one, Portmore Park Farm, which fronted the High Street, being demolished in 1912 to provide the land. The new building was opened on 8 February 1914 and included a mail sorting room, a telegraph room and a telephone exchange.

In the early 1990s the post office was closed and the services were relocated to 30 Church Street, opposite the library building. The mail sorting service is still carried on at the back of the building, but the former post office has been converted into business premises.

Fourteen

Education

Before the direct intervention of government in education provision from the 1870s, most children had a very basic education provided by a few charity or Dame Schools. From the Middle Ages some elementary education was provided through the Chantry schools founded by religious orders, the forerunner of our modern-day grammar schools. Primary schools were normally associated with the village church and the local priest ran the classes which were often held on church property. Only the wealthy could afford to employ private tutors. When Henry VIII dissolved the monasteries in the late 1530s, the Chantry schools disappeared and thereafter education was in the hands of those private individuals whose charitable desire it was to educate the very poor.

With the onset of the Industrial Revolution from the 18th century there was a need for a better educated workforce and it became apparent that intervention was necessary to organise a more systematic education for all sections of the community, regardless of their social background. In the 1780s the Sunday School movement was started, and in 1833 the Government introduced grants for schools. Real change came in 1870 with the Elementary Education Act introduced by Forster. Further Acts of Parliament in the 1870s and '80s made it compulsory for children to learn the 3 Rs and for children younger than 13 years to attend school. From 1889 county councils were able to charge a penny on the rates to construct technical colleges. The Balfour Education Act of 1902 and the Fisher Act of 1918 established county councils as education authorities and raised the school leaving age to 14 years. The Butler Education Act of 1944 established primary and secondary schools in place of elementary schools.

Schools in the voluntary sector became controlled and aided by the state.

Weybridge Dame School

The very first school in the area was founded by Francis Drake of Esher in 1634 for 'the teaching of eighteen poore scholars in the school house that I have built upon the Manors of Walton viz. twelve of Walton and six of Esher'. However, the earliest recorded school to exist in Weybridge was a Dame School held in the present-day Old School Cottages in Baker Street from *c*.1650. The building accommodated 12 boys and girls, who sat for their classes in the same room divided by a low screen. It originally had a thatched roof which was retiled around 1820. It sustained some damage in the Second World War and was under threat of demolition in the mid–1960s, but it was saved by a public outcry and is now private cottages.

98 Watercolour of the Old School in Baker Street, *c*.1880.

95

99 Photographed at the Old School Cottage, Baker Street, *c.*1890, is Mrs. New surrounded by her eldest son, on the left, youngest son on the right, his son (only cousin of Mrs. Alice Booker), an unidentified woman and a dog. Originally there was a label on the reverse which said that it was 'Presented to Weybridge Museum by Mrs. Alice Booker in June 1972 in memory of her grandmother, Mrs. New, who lived at School Cottage for a great many years.' Mrs. New died in 1921. Mrs. Booker lived there in 1905 and 1906.

Hopton Charity School

Hopton Charity School was founded by Elizabeth Hopton in August 1732 after she received consent to build on enclosed land in Loom Pit Lane, for 'the education of poor children'. In a document of 1739 Charles Hopton esquire of Littleton, Middlesex, endowed the Hopton Charity School the sum of £100. In the 1790s the Weybridge Vestry minutes record that five children from the workhouse should be sent to Thomas Simmons' school for their education, which was the Hopton Charity School. Simmons remained as the schoolmaster until 1813, when the parish took over the school. Simmons was also parish and vestry clerk and was paid an annual pension of £50. His son-in-law, Stephen Parsons, later took over the running of the school.

Weybridge Sunday School

During the late 1780s and '90s the Sunday School movement came into being to discipline and teach children on the only day they had off work; many children worked on the farms or in the new expanding industries. Robert Raikes founded the first school at Gloucester in 1780 and the movement gradually spread across the country thereafter.

Weybridge acquired a Sunday School in 1794, which was held near the parish church of St Nicholas. William Hunter was the master and was paid 5s. a day. The children attended from 9 a.m. until midday, then from 2-5 p.m. In 1794 there were 67 boys and 34 girls. All expenses were met by public subscription, with the largest amount coming from the Duchess of

York who subscribed £10, followed by £4 from the Earl and Countess of Portmore and £1 1s. from the Rev. Francis Haultain, rector of St Nicholas' Church.

Weybridge Parochial School

This school was started in 1813 after the Vestry took over responsibility for the Sunday School; it met in the schoolrooms of the Hopton Charity School. It was patronised by the Duke and Duchess of York until the death of the Duchess in 1820. Subscribers were encouraged to visit the school to see the good work being undertaken. This constant visiting must have annoyed the school teachers and interfered with the running of the school, as the headmaster was later to testify in the school logbook. The children entered the school between the ages of five and twelve and attended between 9 a.m. and midday, and from 2-5 p.m. On Sundays they also attended between 10 a.m.-2 p.m. for religious instruction. They were directed to 'behave respectfully to their teachers; to take care of their books and slates; to conduct themselves with reverence during Divine Service; to be kind to one another, and never to tell a lie, cheat, steal or swear'.

These rules were laid down by the Parochial School Committee under the chairmanship of the Rev. Doctor Bell, the school being attached to the Church of England. The first headmaster was Mr. John Tubb, who was employed at a salary of £75 per annum, as well as a rent-free house, and abstained from corporal punishment of the children.

In 1814, 65 boys and 51 girls were attending the school, which was supported by subscription. By 1817, 130 attended and a decision was taken to admit only children from the parish, because too many children from outside were trying to enter. In 1821 the girls' schoolroom was enlarged. Tradition has it that when children left the school the Duchess of York presented the boys with a tool-kit and the girls with a linen box. Between 1826-40 numbers declined, falling from a figure of 138 pupils in 1826-7 to 75 in 1840-1. However, after the arrival of the London and Southampton Railway

in 1838 numbers increased. In 1847 Mr. Tubb resigned and duly received a pension.

By the 1830s provision was made for grant aid to local schools to encourage them to increase their numbers of pupils from the local community. From 1833 grants were distributed through two agencies, the British Society and the National Society. In 1849 Weybridge School applied for a grant of £350 to help build a new schoolroom which was opened in 1852 when Mr. King was appointed teacher. At the time the school had 56 boys and 48 girls attending. Mr. King was supported by pupil-teachers, children above the age of 13 taught by Mr. King to teach the younger pupils. After five years of teaching experience the pupil teachers could apply for a scholarship which would enable them to attend college and eventually become teachers in their own right. By 1860 there were 198 children and a new classroom was built—which did little to satisfy the educational needs of the school.

At this time grants were made to schools on condition the exam results were good and the school was in a fair condition. By 1869 there were 343 children attending, with an assistant mistress teaching the infants. As time progressed the school was split into different classes for boys, girls and infants. Fees were 3d. for the first child from a family, 2d. for the second, and 1d. for book stock.

Weybridge National School

In 1870 the Parochial School became a National School under the Education Act. The boys' department adopted local customs such as May-pole dancing and hot cross buns at Easter. On 25 June each year the school observed St James' Day by attending a special service in the church, followed by tea in a field adjoining the school playground.

In 1890 there were 161 boys in the school under Mr. King, and when he retired in that year Alfred G. Harrison took over. In the same year the Government ended the 'Payment by Results' scheme and awarded the school 10s. per child. In 1891 Mr. Brown was appointed headmaster and worked at the school for the next 25 years. During his tenure a new school was built

100   Weybridge National School, Standard 1 Class, 1894. The boy second from the left in the third row was Brooker, who was to become chief of the Weybridge Fire Brigade. The boy third from the right in the front row was a member of the Newman family who ran a coal business in the village.

in 1894 and the curriculum was changed. After 1902 the school was known as the Weybridge Church of England School, and in 1909 it won three shields in the Surrey Music Competition and in 1910 received a glowing report from the school inspectors. In 1914 the school was used as temporary accommodation for troops on their way to Pirbright and Aldershot soon after the outbreak of the First World War. Mr. Brown died in 1917, when 279 boys were on the roll. Food shortages caused by the German submarine blockade in 1918 led the Weybridge Food Economy Committee to provide school dinners for the boys.

Mr. Brooker replaced Brown as the head-master and during his time the school excelled at sports, mainly football and rifle shooting. When he died in 1929 the school was being run along public school lines, divided into four houses. Mr. Hyde took over as headmaster in 1931 and

remained at the school for the duration of the Second World War. Boys continued to take their swimming lessons in the River Thames and played sport on the Churchfield recreation ground during the war years, as their usual facilities were dug up for allotments. Under the Butler Education Act of 1944 the school became a voluntary controlled body and was renamed St James's Church of England Secondary School.

The school established a separate girls' department in 1869 and the first headmistress was Miss Northam, employed on a salary of £60 per annum. In 1877 the school had 72 girls attending classes and Miss Jackson took over as the head-mistress. At the same time the school started to receive its water from the local water company rather than from a hand pump in the school yard. By 1879 there were 118 girls attending and new subjects, such as cooking and sewing, were introduced to the curriculum. When the boys' school was built in 1894 their former classrooms were occupied by the girls. Miss Hubard was headmistress of the girls' school from 1894 until she retired in 1921. She was a strict disciplinarian and imposed a Victorian culture in the classroom which only ended when a new headmistress, Miss Grant, replaced her. The St James' Girls' Club was started and won the Banner for Singing at the Wimbledon Music Festival in 1926. Ten years later Miss Grant was replaced by Miss English, who stayed at the school until after the Second World War. During the war the school was hit by a bomb, fortunately out of school hours, which blew the school piano halfway up Baker Street, as well as littering the town with text books. The bomb destroyed two classrooms.

The infants' school was set up from 1870. The children sat on simple wooden benches. At the start there were 41 pupils and the first head-mistress was Miss Boys. She was followed by Miss Richardson in 1872. Mrs. Rose, wife of Canon Rose, the rector of St James's Church,

101 A group of women teachers photographed outside St James's School in the 1880s.

102 School children outside St James's in 1913.

often attended the school, helping with reading and writing. Miss Burt took over the infants' school from 1877 and stayed for 40 years until she left in 1917. The inspectors' reports from the 19th century make interesting reading:

> Children are not taught to make proper use of their desks, or to sit in their proper positions for writing, and their habits of answering out of their turn, or of looking over their neighbours' slates must be carefully checked.

But school life was not just one of discipline and the children were allowed to play in the fields when the weather was fine. By 1903, 196 infants attended the school. Miss Burt was replaced by Miss Jenkins in 1917, and under her direction the children learnt to dance and play music. In 1934 Miss Fleming took over the infants; she remained at the school throughout the war years, until she resigned in 1951 to be replaced by Mrs. Puttick.

In 1966 the secondary school was moved to a new building near Weybridge Heath and the school renamed Heathside School. The infants' and junior school later moved to a new site on land purchased from *Oatlands Park Hotel* off Grotto Road. The old buildings were demolished in 1986 and the site redeveloped.

Dr. Spyers School

This school was opened in 1864 by the Rev. Dr. Spyers at Holstein House, High Street, for young gentlemen. Mr. Cottereau later replaced Dr. Spyers, and when he retired he was replaced by Mr. Pike. The school was relocated to Barham Lodge, Oatlands, and in 1867 became a boarding and day school. Holstein House was demolished around 1900, and Barham Lodge in 1964.

St Charles Roman Catholic School

A school connected to the St Charles Borromeo Church in Heath Road was started in 1881 with Jane Donnersback as the headmistress, and 15 children aged from 4-11 years, some of whom arrived by train. Mary E. Duggan was headmistress in 1882 and the building was enlarged in 1883-5 and became eligible for a grant once it was approved by a government

inspection. In 1888 a report criticised the school for its lack of discipline and poor standards. From 1888 Miss Toft took over and started to improve matters, and Father McDaniel left after one visit much impressed by the new condition. In 1893 a cricket club was started by the senior boys. Miss Brown replaced Miss Toft in 1894 and remained until 1900, when Miss Eugenie Driaux took up the position. In 1903 cookery classes were introduced. A year later Miss Norah Brown came to the school and remained until 1936.

In 1909 the building was repainted and gas laid on, and in 1910 a new school was constructed which opened in 1911. When Miss Brown retired in 1936 she was replaced by Miss M.G. Bayley and, later, Miss H.M. Beadle, who remained at the school during the Second World War. At this time there were 59 children attending. School dinners were begun in 1943. By 1968 over 107 children were attending classes.

St George's College

This was another Roman Catholic school, opened at Woburn Park in 1876 by the Josephite Fathers, a religious order from Belgium. They had started a boys' school in Croydon in 1869 but moved in 1876 to Weybridge where the school was built on land purchased from Monsignor W. Petrie. The junior school was housed in the 'Red' house while the seniors were in the 'White' house. In 1912 the boys were examined under the Oxford Local Examinations Board, and a laboratory was set up.

During the First World War a cadet corps was established at the school and after the Armistice a Requiem Mass was held for those boys who had been killed on active service in the armed forces. By 1932 there were 201 boys on the roll.

During the Second World War the school playing fields and grounds were widely used by the Home Guard and the children of schools evacuated from London. Many masters had already joined up by early 1940. In 1943 the school gates and railings were to be confiscated by the government for the war effort, but Father

George Kean successfully appealed for the preservation of the gates, which had originally come from Oatlands Palace. During the war the government allowed the growing and cultivation of tobacco plants, to everybody's great delight.

In 1957 a new school chapel was built to replace an earlier wooden one constructed at the time of Monsignor W. Petrie. Since then the school has expanded dramatically. In 1999 St George's purchased St Mary's Convent.

St Maur's Convent

The third Roman Catholic school to be established in Weybridge was St Maur's Convent School in 1898. This was started by the Sisters of the Holy Infant Jesus who originated from 17th-century France and came to England in 1897. In 1898 the Sisters moved into Clinton House and renamed the house St Maur's Convent. Education followed the French model. The girls' uniform consisted of white blouses and long blue skirts in the winter and an all-white uniform in the summer. In 1938 there were 77 girls on the roll and by 1945 the number had increased to 411. Over the years additional buildings have been added to the school including a chapel, gym and extra classrooms. The St Maur's sisters also ran a kindergarten which moved to new accommodation in 1957.

The Hall School

This famous school was founded by Miss E.V. Gilpin in 1898 in the village hall on the corner of Prince's Road. Miss Gilpin brought quite a radical and fresh approach to teaching which was in stark contrast to the methods used in the Victorian schools of the day. She encouraged children to seek out information for themselves and she helped to create a lively independent spirit in her pupils. The school was divided into three houses, Whigs, Discoverers and Greenflies, and each house had to put on a school play every year on a topic of their own choosing. She also ran history competitions and encouraged the children to give illustrated talks on topics they found of interest. Pupils were also allocated jobs within the school and were encouraged to be critical of each other's work. Margaret Le Fevre, writing in 1968, described these methods:

> All subjects taught at the school favoured part of whatever topic was the main theme at any particular time, described in an inspection report of 1926 as a lively 'Liberal Education'. It is described as a completeness in the spirit and work of the pupils and of their teachers, manifestations of a life intelligent and ordered. The children are happy, with teachers able to take their share in a very perfect system of education with a Headmistress whose genius and devotion have inspired and sustained the supreme purposes of education.

103 St Maur's School in Thames Street, *c.*1924.

104 Children in a classroom in The Hall School, 1930s. This clearly illustrates the alternative and informal teaching methods adopted by the headmistress, Miss Gilpin.

Games took place in a field next to Wallop School in Churchfield Road. Tennis, croquet, rounders, lacrosse and netball were all played by the girls. Regular school trips were made to historic sites such as Westminster Abbey. The school had 100 children aged from 5-15 years of age. When Miss Gilpin retired in 1934 she was replaced by Miss Brooks. During the Second World War the school was evacuated to Bralton Seymour, Somerset, where it remained after 1945.

Wallop School

This school was founded by Mr. Roper-Spyers, the grandson of Dr. Spyers who founded the school at Holstein House in the 1860s. Wallop is the name of the estate Mr. Roper-Spyers had at Nether Wallop in Hampshire. He had been an Anglican priest and also an actor before he founded the school above a shop in Church Street. At first he had seven boys attending classes. When the numbers increased he held classes in a house in Hanger Hill called 'Springfield'. A new school was built in Baker Street, which was sold in 1917 to the Royal Masonic Institute. Afterwards the school was purchased by a Mr. Roper, who was no relation, and the school was then moved to a house called 'Hillcrest' on Monument Hill, but it later returned to 'Springfield', where it has remained ever since. Mr. Roper was headmaster of the school until 1946 when he sold it to Colonel Bliss, who took over as headmaster. Colonel Bliss remained at the school until 1975 when it was sold to another headmaster, Mr. J.D.G. Hewitt. When

Mr. Hewitt died in 1985, his brother, E.M.G. Hewitt, became the proprietor of the school but did not teach there. The school remained in the Hewitt family until it closed in 1999.

Royal Masonic Junior School for Girls

As mentioned above, Dr. Roper-Spyers sold the Wallop School building in Baker Street to the Royal Masonic Institute in 1917 and they founded the Royal Masonic Junior School for Girls in 1918. Miss Harrop was the first headmistress and there were 45 girls on the roll. In 1924 it had 120 children and a new wing was added to accommodate the growing numbers. During the Second World War staff and pupils moved out and Unilever occupied the premises. The school moved back in 1946 with Miss Vaughan as headmistress. In 1947 a gymnasium was added, as well as a craft room and tennis courts. It closed in 1974 and the site is now occupied by the Hill Crest housing estate.

Oakfield Kindergarten

This school was founded by Miss Barnard in Dorchester Road in November 1939 and provided childcare for youngsters aged between 4 and 7 years. Later on, children aged from 3½ years were taken in. The kindergarten provided a useful service during the war, when it allowed mothers to deposit their children in the nursery while they went off to do war work in one of the many local factories. After 1957 the kindergarten just looked after younger children, in the 3½ to 5 years range.

Weybridge Park College

This school was located in Weybridge Park House, off Hanger Hill. The house itself was built in 1867 by Charles Churchill, who established a very comfortable house there. Some time after his death in 1905 the house was converted into a Catholic boys' school, known as Weybridge Park College, which survived until the early 1920s. In June 1926 the property was sold to Mr. E.H. Thompson who pulled down a third of the house and developed the site. Later, the building was converted into a hotel which in turn was demolished in 1975-6.

Weybridge Technical Institute

This was opened on 7 November 1912 by the education department of Surrey County Council for the technical training of children from elementary schools, boys in woodworking and girls in domestic science. It was joint funded by the County and Weybridge Councils and was built by S.J. Love of Sunningdale at a cost of £4,840. Mrs. Hilda Vaughan, a lifelong resident of Oatlands, remembers going to the girls' classes at the Technical Institute:

> For domestic science we used to have to walk down to Weybridge Technical, and we had three courses down there, one course was laundry, the next one was cooking and the next one was housewifery. We learned to clean fenders for great big stoves, and scrub tables, and for the laundry we used to be able to take something every week and wash and iron. We got down there about 9 o'clock and got home by 12 o'clock, I think. Once we got down there and no teacher was there, so we all turned around and came back again and then, when

105 The Technical Institute in Weybridge photographed soon after it opened in November 1912.

106 Rear view of Heath House, *c*.1920. This private property was later converted into a girls' school and then a hotel.

we got back again, we found that we had to go back again and all the time we walked you see. We didn't have buses to take us back again; we had to walk backwards and forwards. The main thing about it was, in Bakers Street they had a baker's shop and we went in and got two-penny-worth of stale cakes, and that was a bag full at that time. But we thoroughly enjoyed going to the Technical College.

The Technical College is now used as an Adult Education centre.

Heath House School

Heath House School was located in the former home of the Scott family, who had built the house in 1854. After the First World War the house was converted into a girls' school, and was known thereafter as Heath House School. The school finally closed in 1945, and the house became a hotel. By 1987 the hotel had closed and a successful campaign was launched to save the property from demolition.

Fifteen

Leisure and Pleasure

Ever since the middle of the 18th century, people have come to the Weybridge area, drawn by the rural nature of the locality. The countryside here offered the visitor a retreat from the hustle and bustle of the metropolis, only a short coach journey from Weybridge. In the early 1800s the Georgian actress Fanny Kemble likened the appearance of the area, especially around Oatlands Park, to America—a name that appeared on Ordnance Survey maps until the early 20th century.

After the coming of the railway in 1838, the area retained its rural charm for many years, despite the encroachment of bricks and mortar. The surrounding heathland and countryside provided plenty of scope for walking and rambling. Miss H.M. Tiley fondly remembered walking in the Weybridge district in the early 1900s when she wrote:

> There were lots of nice walks, a favourite one was over the Wey Bridge and along the canal bank, past the watercress beds, to New Haw, then turn left across some fields and over the railway lines and along by a lake belonging to Mr. Locke King, used for private fishing, then over a little wooden bridge where the River Wey went under the seven-arched railway bridge, then by footpath to Weybridge station and so home in Station Road (later called Hanger Hill). Another walk was across Chertsey Meads to Chertsey Bridge, a lovely open space, with plenty of room to run about, skylarks singing, and once we found a nest with eggs in it, just a little grassy ring, not really a nest. Then another way was along by the River Wey to the Oil Mill and over a bridge by the lock where the Wey runs into the Thames, that was a popular fishing place, all along the

tow path from the bridge. Then along Jessamy Road to Thames Street and down to the Thames river. On these walks we always picked bunches of wild flowers. St George's Hill attracted many people but it was a long walk up to the Swiss Cottage where we could get some tea, which was always welcome.

Literature, Theatre, Cinema

Many writers and poets drew inspiration from the Weybridge area, particularly in the 19th century. As we have already seen, Fanny Kemble wrote about her childhood in the area while living at 'Eastlands', and the diarist Grenville wrote about the Yorks at Oatlands Park. George Meredith lived at 'The Limes' from 1848-53 and was inspired by the surrounding woods and commons, especially St George's Hill. Meredith struck up a close friendship with Janet Duff Gordon, the daughter of Sir Alexander Duff Gordon, who lived nearby at 'Nutfield Cottage'. They often went on long walks together, and in her old age Janet referred to Meredith as 'my poet'.

Robert Louis Stevenson (1850-94) stayed at the *Hand and Spear Hotel* in 1881, correcting the proofs for *Treasure Island*, published in 1882. Stevenson wrote to his friend Lloyd Osbourne about his time in Weybridge:

> My mouth was empty, there being not one word more of *Treasure Island* in my bosom and here were the proofs of the beginning already waiting for me at the *Hand and Spear*. There I corrected them, living for the most part alone, walking on the Heath at Weybridge in the dewy Autumn mornings, a good deal pleased with what I had done.

107 The Victorian poet George Meredith with his son, Arthur, in 1864.

The small Davenport desk at which Stevenson worked was given to Weybridge Museum in 1968 by the then licensee of the *Hand and Spear*, Miss E. Carlyle.

Emile Zola, author of *La Bête Humaine* and *Germinal*, lived for a while in 1898 in Weybridge, after fleeing France at the height of the Dreyfus Affair. Zola had come to England to escape imprisonment after the publication of his famous article, 'J'Accuse', in which he defended the Jewish French Army officer, Dreyfus, against charges of spying for Germany. He journeyed to London where he stayed at the *Grosvenor Hotel*. Fearing that he would be recognised, he left for *Oatlands Park Hotel*, where he stayed with his friend Desmoulin. He then rented a house called 'Penn', at 24 Oatlands Chase, where he settled down to write his novel, *Fecondite*. At the time he was using the false name of 'Jacques Beauchamp'. On 27 August 1898 he moved to a house at 17 Summerfields, Spinney Hill,

Addlestone, where he was joined by his mistress, Jeanne Rozet and their children. Five months later Zola left for France after receiving a pardon from the French Government.

Another author connected with the area was E.M. Forster, who lived at 'Harnham', 19 Monument Green, with his mother. Forster drew much of his inspiration from the characters he knew in Edwardian Weybridge, living here for 21 years until he moved to Abinger, near Guildford.

Warwick Deeping, another 20th-century novelist, lived at 'Eastlands', the old home of the Kemble family. Deeping took to writing after serving with the Royal Army Medical Corps in the First World War. He came to Weybridge in 1919 and in 1925 published *Sorrell and Son*. For the next 20 years he published many romantic stories, some of which have also been made into successful films. His wife, Maude, opened the grounds of their family home after Warwick Deeping died in 1971.

The Weybridge Theatre, which operated from about 1751 until 1800, was a single-storey building, barn-like in appearance, with an ornate façade fronting onto Baker Street. It was used for all manner of public assemblies, ranging from one-night plays to Methodist meetings. One group of players was led by Mr. William Smith, who retired in 1797. A London-based actor-manager, Mr. Henry Thornton, took over the running of the theatre after being appointed by the Duchess of York, who patronised the Weybridge Theatre. Thornton died in 1799 and his gravestone records that he had performed before Frederick, Prince of Wales, in 1751. The theatre languished around 1800 and was bought by Lady Tuite, who turned it into two tene-ments. In 1822 it was sold again to Robert Hyde, a Weybridge baker. The building was demolished in 1900 when Baker Street was widened.

Public performances later took place in Holstein Hall, which was built by John Wiltshire, a local caterer, in the grounds of Holstein House in 1904. It was designed by Henry Budd and built by local builder, William Mann & Co. It could seat 900 people and opened on 7 January 1905. After the First World War the hall fell into decline, its wealthier clients going up to St George's Hill Golf Club. During the war it was purchased by Vickers for use as an aircraft factory. It was bought by Douglas Cleland in 1923 and converted into a billiards hall, although it failed the same year. It was subsequently bought by Mr. S.H. Wood who converted it into a motor garage which opened for business in 1924. The hall had various uses until it was demolished in the 1960s and replaced with shops.

The Victorian music-hall and comic character, Ally Sloper, was created by Weybridge resident Charles Henry Ross. Ross lived at 21 Jessamy Road, and became editor of *Judy* magazine in about 1869. The magazine was a weekly cartoon strip, the Victorian equivalent of *The Beano*. His French wife, Marie Duval, was a gifted cartoonist who finished off his rough sketches for publication. Their creation, Ally Sloper, was a tall thin character who poked his nose into other people's business and wisecracked at the expense of some of the highest in the land, including the monarchy. He was the first British comic cartoon character. A million copies of the magazine and a book were published in 1873. *Ally Sloper's Half Holiday* was published weekly at 1d. a copy from 1884 until 1949; comic souvenirs were also produced, including clay pipes, neck ties, tobacco jars, whisky and gold watches. The Ally Sloper character appeared alongside Lord Billy, Ikey Moses, Ma Sloper, Auntie, Miss Golightly and even Snatcher the Dog. The Victorian actor, Austin Melford, appeared on stage

as Ally Sloper, and a photograph of him was taken by the studio photographers Brown Barnes Bell around 1885. Elmbridge Museum has in its collection a brick with an Ally Sloper clay pipe embedded in it found by a workman during the demolition of Finnart House in Weybridge in 1981. The museum also has an oil painting of Charles Henry Ross in 1897, the year he died.

The cinema began to make an impact in the area in the early 1900s. Walton-on-Thames had acquired a film industry under the inspiration of Cecil Hepworth from 1900, and its first cinema around 1915-16. Weybridge's first cinema was opened in Queen's Parade, Church Street in 1920. The parade had originally been built by Mr. Horace Thompson in 1899 and the premises were used by the Gordon Watney Engineering Company during the First World War. In 1927 the cinema was refitted by W.G. Tarrant to seat 500 people and in 1929 it was sold to the County Cinema chain who called it the King George's Cinema. The first 'talkie' films were shown there at that time. Later, in 1937, the name was changed to the County Cinema. It survived until the early 1950s when it was converted into a public hall by the Council. The second cinema was in Queen's Road, opening in 1934 as the Odeon. It survived until 1960, when it was converted into a Catholic church, St Martin De Pores, which opened in 1964. The church stayed in the building until the late 1980s when it was demolished and modern shops were built on the site.

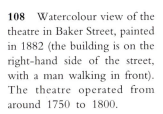
108 Watercolour view of the theatre in Baker Street, painted in 1882 (the building is on the right-hand side of the street, with a man walking in front). The theatre operated from around 1750 to 1800.

109 Maypole dancing in Bull Ring Square, Monument Green, *c.*1750.

Sport

Many forms of leisure activity in the village centred around the public houses, but open public spaces such as Monument Green were also important. Elmbridge Museum has a beautiful panel oil painting dating from *c.*1750 which shows Maypole dancing, reputedly at the *Ship Inn*. The panel was found in 1914 and given to the museum by Mrs. Charles Routh, who lived at Lavender Cottage (once known as Monument House), Monument Green. The panel depicts figures playing music, drinking and dancing. There are also a number of signatures scratched onto the surface, which correspond to some of the figures depicted. The style is of the English naïve school, probably by a self-taught artist. The figures have a comic quality, as if the artist were painting a satire on Weybridge life. We shall probably never know the true origins of this panel painting.

In 1908 Weybridge Council opened Churchfields recreation ground off Church Street, next to St James's. The gates and park were donated by Mr. John Lyle of the Tate and Lyle Sugar Company, who lived at Finnart House. A tree was planted in the recreation ground in July 1911, to celebrate the coronation of George V, by the eldest resident of Weybridge, Mr. Deverant, who was 100 years old at the time. The recreation ground has been used for sporting and social activities ever since.

By 1900 there were two cricket clubs in Weybridge, the Albion and the St Michael's Church teams. The Albion Club charged members a 5s. subscription. It was the older of the two and has certainly been operating since the 1870s. However, other teams played in the area too. A poster dated 30 May 1882 advertises a cricket match that was to be

> played on Weybridge Common between 12 Gentlemen of Weybridge (selected by the Committee of Oatlands Park Cricket Club) and 12 Players of Weybridge (selected by the Committee of the Weybridge Albion Cricket Club).

The wickets were 'pitched punctually' at 11 o'clock. The cricket ground was 'improved' by providing seating, and lime trees which were planted by Mr. Henry Yool of Oakfield, later Field Place, a notable citizen and chairman of Surrey County Council. When he died a memorial was erected on the corner of Oatlands Drive; it was moved in the 1970s to the junction of Hanger Hill and Prince's Road. The inscription reads, 'Erected by the Parishioners in memory of Henry Yool of Field Place, Weybridge, 1896'.

Prior to 1914 the Albion cricket team was in a very prosperous state. Captained at that time by Mr T. Bowman, the club held charity matches, which were only discontinued in 1921. Harry Anstead was a well-known Albion player who

110 Cricket team at Weybridge Common in *c*.1890.

111 This highly amusing postcard shows a display by the 3rd Dragoon Guards at the Weybridge Sports Day on Whit Monday in 1909. This is one of a series of four postcards in the collections at Elmbridge Museum showing different displays by the Guards at the Weybridge Sports Day in 1909.

won many cups for his batting. Another successful team at that time was the Weybridge Electricity Company team, which played in the Woking and District Cricket League. They won the league in 1921, and afterwards held a celebratory dinner in the *Hare and Hounds Hotel*. Three years later a joint decision was made by the two remaining Weybridge teams, the Albion and the Electric Company, to merge and form the Weybridge Cricket Club. The first match was played on 24 May 1924 against the Vickers Cricket Club. Since then, Weybridge Cricket Club has gone from strength to strength, with many memorable matches played. The Second World War interrupted activities, but the club is still a firmly established sporting feature of the village.

In the early years of the 20th century golfing became a popular pastime for the local gentry and the middle classes. The St George's Hill Golf Course was opened just before the First World War on land developed by W.G. Tarrant. It was designed by Mr. Harry S. Colt, a professional golf-course designer. The course was perhaps Colt's masterpiece. Work started in 1912 on clearing the forest of pine trees that covered The Hill. These had been planted from the 18th century to improve the barren hill top, work inspired by the Rev. Joseph Spence of Byfleet. The clearance work involved the use of a steam traction engine, teams of horses, and many labourers, whose job it was to cut down the trees, clear out the roots and remove all the felled timber. A series of postcards was issued at the time showing the work being carried out.

Dynamite was sometimes used to blow up the roots of the larger trees.

The course was constructed in less than two years. A clubhouse with a thatched roof was also built, much of the timber for its construction coming from the trees felled on the course, and it is probable that most of the bricks came from local brickworks at Claygate and Oxshott. By 7 June 1913 the course and adjoining clubhouse were ready for opening by His Serene Highness Prince Alexander of Teck, the club president. He was Queen Mary's brother and was later to become the Earl of Athlone. *Golfing* magazine of 8 October 1913 described the new course:

The new golf course at St George's Hill, Weybridge, was opened with more than *eclat*. The course, beautifully planned on the St George's Hill estate, is laid out on an extensive scale, and for its picturesque character alone is likely to become famous. It is 6,300 yards long, the holes of a good average length, winding in and out of the finely-wooded land. The outward and homeward halves take the form of large loops, the ninth and eighteenth greens being opposite the club-house. For the opening, twelve of the leading professionals in England engaged in a medal round for money prizes amounting in the aggregate to £100 in the morning, while in the afternoon a team of the Oxford and Cambridge Golfing Society, got together by Mr. A.C.M. Croome, opposed the professionals in foursome play, receiving two holes for each pair. Mr. Horace Hutchinson, the Captain of the Club, who was to have driven the first ball, was unfortunately indisposed, so that the honour of so driving fell on W.I. Ritchie, who with C.H. Mayo formed the first pair.

The clubhouse was burnt down on 18 March 1920 and was rebuilt without its thatched roof. Between the two wars the course achieved its greatest fame and was patronised by royalty, with the Prince of Wales accepting captaincy of the club in 1934-5. His brother, the Duke of York, later King George VI, was also fond of the club. Perhaps the most infamous visitor ever to enter the clubhouse was Nazi Foreign Minister, Von Ribbenthrop, a guest in 1937. He had come to Britain to attend the coronation of King George VI on 12 May 1937. He was heavily criticised in the press for appearing to give a Nazi salute to the crowds watching him pass by in his offical motor car, when in London.

During the Second World War the club continued to play, but the second course (opened in the late 1920s) was turned over to the forces and barrage balloons were placed across the site to prevent German bombers attacking the Vickers aircraft factory at Brooklands. Anti-aircraft gun emplacements were also erected, one being put on the seventh green. Troops were billeted at the clubhouse, and the roof was used as an air-craft observation post by the army. In the 1950s the club slowly recovered from the effects of the war, and by the 1960s had regained something of its old style. However, as far as the social scene was concerned the heyday for the club was in the 1920s-30s.

The St George's Hill Lawn Tennis Club was opened on 7 June 1913 by His Serene Highness Prince Alexander of Teck, the same day as the Golf Club. The club had eight grass courts, two hard courts, two crocquet lawns, and a bowling green. A lake nearby was stocked with trout and used for boating and fishing. The club-house was again thatched and it suffered the same fate as its neighbour, burning down in March 1918. It was rebuilt and re-opened on 25 July 1921. Since then the club has attracted a wide range of professional and amateur players including several Wimbledon tennis champions such as Bjorn Borg, who played there just before he won his first Wimbledon title.

Weybridge Rifle Club was founded on 19 April 1901 after a public meeting at the village hall decided it would be in the best interests of the village if the men were proficient in the handling of firearms. This was the time of the Boer War, which had already shown up the poor marksmanship of the regular British Army against their Boer opponents. Mr. Pilditch had called the meeting, and land suitable for a range was donated to the club by Hugh Locke King. The meeting was chaired by the rector of St James's Church, the Rev. W.B. Money, who praised the patriotism of the many rifle clubs already established throughout the country. He spoke of the crisis that had arisen as a result of the Boer War and how Britain was isolated from the international community because of it. Germany in particular was very hostile to British actions in South Africa, and used the tension between the two countries to expand its navy. Hugh Locke King, who was elected president of the new Weybridge Rifle Club, was aware of these tensions. The club was supported by the local gentry who subsidised the shooting activities of the working-class members. In November 1902 the club had its first annual dinner and membership had reached 200 people. With the building of the Brooklands racing circuit in 1906-7 the range was moved to the other side of the main railway line, nearer Weybridge village.

In the 18th century the rivers Thames and Wey were used for pleasure by the local gentry and aristocracy. It was not until more recently, however, that organised watersports became a feature of life in the area. In the early 20th century Weybridge had a regatta, something which was common on the Thames at this time. The first regatta held in England occurred on the Thames near Westminster Bridge in 1775. On 7 August of that year the Duke of Newcastle held a regatta upstream from Walton Bridge opposite Oatlands Park estate. The *Gentleman's Magazine* recorded that there was 'displayed a magnificent regatta at Oatlands at which were present His Royal Highness The Prince of Wales and Princess Amelia'. Since then, virtually every town along a 15-mile stretch of the river has

113 A tennis party in Weybridge, *c*.1921.

114 St James's School rifle club, *c*.1910.

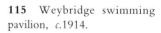

115 Weybridge swimming pavilion, *c*.1914.

had a regatta. A *Surrey Herald* reporter wrote of a 1912 event:

> From Bell Weir Lock to Sunbury Lock, embracing the banks running by Staines, Laleham, Chertsey, Weybridge, and Walton, there has been one long moving procession of craft of all shapes and sizes. The call of the river brought forth crowds of habitués to seek the enjoyment that is derived from the delightful pastime in this popular part of the Thames Valley.

The Weybridge regatta continued annually until the First World War, after which it went into decline. On 27 June 1930 the *Surrey Herald* reported that it had been dropped owing to a lack of interest.

By the turn of the 20th century public bathing had become a very fashionable pastime. A public bathing place had been established on the Thames at Weybridge by 1903 and the council employed a bathing attendant, Sergeant E. Linwood. He had previously been employed by the Cape Mounted Police. Public swimming was allowed from 6 a.m. until 12 noon, and from 4 p.m. until dusk. The bathing place was reserved for the use of ladies from 10 a.m. until 1 p.m. There was a national sensation in 1911 when Weybridge Council allowed mixed bathing in the Thames. An article in the *Daily Telegraph* in June 1911 reported that the bathing superintendent had said:

> Mixed bathing has proved very successful and as soon as more people get to know about it we shall get even more here. I believe some of the ladies are still a little diffident about it, but I think that they will soon get over their nervousness and come along.

The accommodation provided by the council consisted of 'a little green building standing on the towing path some ten yards from the river, and those desirous of a dip have to walk down to the water along strips of matting'. Schoolchildren also came to learn how to swim in parties of 25 pupils. The council charged 3d. for costumes and 1d. for towels.

Rowing was, and still is, a very popular activity on the Thames. There has been a Weybridge Rowing Club for many years, catering for the men of the district. The Weybridge Ladies Amateur Rowing Club was started in 1926 by local woman Amy Gentry, who had been a member of the Weybridge Rowing Club from 1920. She came to the conclusion that there were enough young women interested in rowing to warrant a separate club in the village for women. The club was so successful that it won the Women's Amateur Sculling Championship Cup in 1930. Women from the club have represented their country in various international competitions, including the Olympics.

Many of the towns and villages in the district had their own football clubs by the beginning of the 20th century and Weybridge was no exception. From the mid-1890s a team played on a piece of ground in Walton Lane. Known as the Weybridge Rose Football Club, the club was so successful that in 1905-6 they were in the second division of the Kingston and District Football League. Members of that team included E. Goree (linesman), A. Millson, A. Holmes, G.A. Bright, A. Crook, A. Radley, E. Nash, W. Beale, W. Stroud, T.F. Bennet (Hon. Secretary) and J. Reed (Vice-Captain). A report in the *Surrey Herald* on 12 October 1912 mentions that club had failed to retain the Surrey Senior Cup, which they won in 1911. The club's senior side had played 30 games in 1912, winning 12, drawing 7 and losing 11. The club also toured on the continent and visited Austria where they played two games against Slavia Sports Club. The club had spent £700 in the last four years (1908-12) improving their ground at Walton Lane, which was also shared with the local athletics club. Mr. Brian Brooker was captain of the first eleven.

Unfortunately, the club went into terminal decline in the period after the First World War, probably as a result of the success of other local clubs such as Hersham and Walton. Weybridge Football Club, as it was then called, was disbanded in July 1930 after losing the use of their ground. The *Surrey Herald* reported on 1 August 1930 that part of the reason for the club's decline was the deplorable apathy in the district to sporting activities. It is probable that the cinema and other forms of leisure had a great impact on sporting activity. Interestingly,

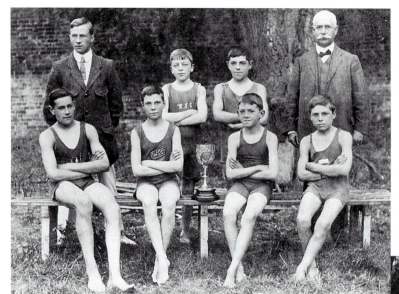

116 Swimmers from St James's School, *c*.1914.

117 Members of the Weybridge Rowing Club, winners of the Desborough Cup, 1927.

118 Members of the Weybridge Ladies Amateur Rowing Club (WLARC) attending a Thames regatta in 1929. Miss Amy Gentry, founder of the club, is standing fourth from left.

119   The Weybridge Rose Football Club, 1905-6.

120   St James's School Football Club, 1910-11.

121 Players from the Weybridge Football Club, *c*.1920.

122 Members of the Weybridge rugby football team in their first season, 1931-2.

Weybridge Post Office also had a football team for a number of years around 1907.

The Weybridge Sports Day was held at the football ground in Walton Lane, and attracted large crowds. The event began in 1906 and by the First World War included a varied programme of track and field events, music, and military displays of various kinds, including the demonstrations by the 3rd Dragoon Guards. At the Sports Day on Whit Monday in 1909, it appears the guards were having a game of football with huge inflatable balls, an amusing way of displaying their horsemanship skills, though what the public thought of this we can only guess.

Hugh Locke King built a motor racing circuit on his estate at Brooklands in 1906-7 after discovering that British racing drivers were losing races on the continent because there was no dedicated racing circuit in this country. He employed a large workforce of navvies to excavate the track, which was 2½ miles long with embankments so steep that people could not stand on them. Lord Montagu called the track 'that grey girdle of concrete'. It was officially opened on 17 June 1907 with a cavalcade of cars led by Ethel Locke King, whose husband could not drive. During the First World War all racing stopped at Brooklands and the circuit was given over to the military. The heyday for the circuit was the inter-war period, dominated by racing men and women like Malcolm Campbell, Kaye Don and Tim Birkin. The last races occurred in late summer 1939, after which the track was closed for the duration of the Second World War as the site was

123 Brooklands, *c.*1908-14, showing the members clubhouse and enclosure.

124 Brooklands, *c.*1908-14, showing the clubhouse and track as seen from the hillside overlooking the course.

used for aircraft production. Legend has it that after the war the track was offered back to the racing fraternity, who declined to use it as it was already outdated. Modern racing cars required a larger circuit and it is likely that racing would almost certainly have stopped at Brooklands by the late 1940s. The track was also used for cycle and motor-cycle racing.

The pioneers of aviation quickly saw the track as a good place for an airstrip and flying schools. Alliott Verdon Roe was the first aviator to fly an aircraft from Brooklands, in 1908. George Holt Thompson persuaded Hugh Locke King to entertain flyers at the motor circuit and thereby boost the popularity of the site. The French pilot Louis Paulhan flew at Brooklands in November 1909. By the following year Charles Rolls, Claude

Grahame-White, Graham Gilmour and Gustav Hamel were all taking to the air. The first flying school to be established was by Charles Lane in 1910, quickly followed by others, including Hewlett and Blondeau, Neale School, Bristol School, Hanriot, Avro, Grahame-White, Ducrocq and Lawford, Deperdussin, Herbert Spencer, Vickers, Sopwith and Bleriot. After the First World War the Brooklands Flying Club was established and successfully taught flying from the late 1920s until the outbreak of the Second World War. After the war the club never resumed its activities at Brooklands, and the site was given over to aircraft manufacture. The story of Brooklands is now told in an excellent museum which relates the fascinating history of motor racing and aviation in Weybridge.

Sixteen

In Time of War

The Weybridge Volunteers

There was some very limited military activity in the Weybridge district following the outbreak of the English Civil War in 1642. The first great threat to domestic peace came with the wars against revolutionary France from 1793 onwards. There was a brief respite in the fighting following the Peace of Amiens in 1803, but within a few months it had erupted again and the threat of invasion gripped the whole nation. Volunteer units were established throughout the country. The government used powers granted by a bill passed in 1798 to expand voluntary regiments to a total strength of 150,000 men. Sleepy Weybridge played its part, particularly as the commander of the British Army, the Duke of York, lived at Oatlands Park. He created his own voluntary regiment whose declaration was:

> We, the Duke of York's Loyal Weybridge Volunteers, having mutually agreed to hold ourselves in readiness (in case of Invasion, Insurrection or the Appearance of an Enemy in Force on the Coast), to act as may be required by His Majesty agreeably to the Acts of Parliament for the Defence of the Nation— do so in the honour bind ourselves, when on Duty, to obey the Commands of our Officers.

The volunteers wore red coats with blue facings, silver lace for the officers and white for the other ranks, and blue trousers.

The regiment first appeared in the List of Volunteers in 27 February 1804, although the first commission was in 1803. The captain of the unit was William Barnett; his lieutenant was Osborn Barwell, with John F. Ewant as ensign. All three men received their commission on

22 September 1803. William Barnett had a poster printed on 5 August 1803 addressed to the 'Men of Weybridge'. The language employed was hardly peaceful, as this extract demonstrates:

> You may be called forth to resent the INSULT you have received—to CHASTISE those, who if they attempt an INVASION of this Country come, according to their insolent boast, to put COWARDS to flight! BRITONS! THIS IS THE BOAST OF FRENCHMEN; and could we insult our own breasts, by harbouring a thought that this taunt was just, and they successful, DREADFUL WOULD BE THE CONSEQUENCE. You will receive ARMS in the sacred cause of your beloved KING, of your RELIGION, of your LAWS—in one Word, of YOUR COUNTRY.

The unit comprised two lieutenants, three sergeants, three corporals, two drummers, and a total strength of 104 men. The soldiers received pay for 20 days' training per year and were expected to march to 'any part of Great Britain for the defence thereof'. They were disbanded in 1805 after the Battle of Trafalgar ended any real threat of an invasion by the French.

The Boer War

During the Boer War (1899-1902) many local men travelled to Kingston upon Thames to enlist in the East Surrey Regiment, which had a barracks there. The residents of Weybridge were caught up in the patriotic fervour of the time, especially after the British Army lifted the Boer siege of Mafeking in 1900, and many shops in High Street were decorated with bunting and flags and banners extolling the fighting prowess

125 A 'Grand Patriotic Procession and Carnival' was held in Weybridge on Thursday 28 June 1900 to celebrate British victories in the South African War. This view shows one of the many floats organised for the event, showing Britannia and children in national costume and uniforms. A member of the Weybridge Fire Brigade stands beside the cart. Note the Chinese lanterns decorating the house in the background.

of the British Army. They read 'Well done to Buller [a British general] and The Surreys [the East Surrey Regiment]', and 'Our Country's Love to You Tommy Atkins'. A Grand Patriotic Procession was held in the village on 28 June 1900 to celebrate this and other British victories in the South African War, and in the parade were many horse-drawn floats, including a clown troupe.

The First World War

The First World War affected the lives of local people far more than any previous war had done. At the start of hostilities with Germany in August 1914 hundreds of young men volunteered for the services, mainly the army, expecting the war to be over by Christmas. No one expected the war to last longer than six months, except for Lord Kitchener, who had predicted that the war with Germany would go on for at least three years.

The first refugees from Belgium flooded into England soon after and some arrived in Weybridge, where they occupied cheap rented accommodation—the rates having been lowered especially. During the war a total of more than 250,000 Belgian refugees came to Britain. They worked in the factories around Weybridge and opened a branch of the Belgian Metalworkers' Union, which worked to protect the rights of refugee war workers employed in factories and

munitions plants in the country from 1917. A man called De Meyer became the president. Most local members of the Union worked at the Vickers aircraft factory at Brooklands.

During the war a Home Guard unit was formed under the auspices of the Weybridge Home Guard Committee, whose chairman was Theodore Morison. It drilled in Holstein Hall on Tuesday and Friday evenings from 8.30 p.m. Anyone wishing to enrol went to the Watney Garage at Addlestone on Wednesday at 3 p.m. or Saturday at 5.30 p.m. The unit appealed for funds to purchase arms, ammunition and uniforms; cheques could be made out to the Weybridge Home Guard or the V.T.C. (Volunteer Training Corps), at the London County and Westminster Banks, Weybridge, and at E.A. Jemmett, Bank House, Weybridge. The unit was established on 14 January 1915 but did not survive the duration of the war. Many houses in the area were immediately requisitioned for use as military hospitals, and in 1915 there was the first air raid alarm, caused by a German Zeppelin.

As the war progressed, older men and young women took over the factory jobs of those who had departed for the Front. From 1916 Germany pressed home her submarine blockade of Britain, resulting in severe food shortages and rationing, and from 1917 large areas of land were dug up and used for growing food, including the

126 'The Watney Lot' photographed at Watneys works, near Addlestone, in 1915.

Churchfields recreation ground. Houses were requisitioned by the army throughout the district for billeting troops, and villagers helped finance the war effort by raising a war loan for the Government of over £265,000. In 1918 a National Kitchen was established and opened in Weybridge by the District Council.

As the casualties mounted on the Western Front, pressure was put on local men to leave the reserved occupations, such as railway workers, engineers and farmers, and to join the colours. Many had already joined the East Surrey Regiment at nearby Kingston upon Thames; from 1914 many more were to join 'The Watney Lot', a company of mechanics and drivers trained by Major Gordon Watney (see page 60). This

became the 244 Motorised Transport Company, which served throughout the war in the Gallipoli campaign and the Balkans. The unit was first formed as the Home Counties Divisional Supply Column, Territorial Army, in August 1914, and trained at Weybridge, Bulford, and Holcombe, Somerset. In 1915 they embarked for the east, landing in Egypt in March, and later travelling to Gallipoli and Mudros in May and Doiran and Monastir in November. They were all evacuated from December 1915 to Salonika, where they remained until 1919 supplying Serbian forces in the Balkans campaign. From its depot in Salonika the company operated 125 lorries, as well as using pack horses for rougher terrain. The unit operated as part of

127 Photograph of 244 (M.T.) Coy, A.S.C., at Holcombe, Somerset on 26 February 1915.

128 St George's Hill Military Hospital, *c*.1915-20. Before the war this building was the St George's Hill golf course clubhouse.

the 29th Divisional Supply Column. The Royal Army Service Corps had 20,000 men in the Balkans, nearly 12 per cent of the total British force, 700 of whom did not return from Macedonia. The first man killed in the company was Private Charles Rigby, who was married and lived at No. 6 Church Walk. He was killed at Gallipoli by a shell.

The 244 M.T. Company was the first unit in the British army to adopt a crest on its vehicles. Their crest was signed in September 1914 and was an adaptation of the Surrey County crest of three fishes. Metal stencils were cut in the unit workshops and applied to vehicles from October 1914. By early 1915 the idea had caught on with other units. Although known officially as 244 Company, the unit was nicknamed 'The Three Fishes Company'.

The guiding light behind the provision of military hospitals staffed by civilian volunteers in the area was Ethel Locke King. She chaired a meeting in Weybridge on 18 August 1914 to organise relief for the wounded troops and to provide hospitals for the war wounded. A War Distress Fund was established. She was also vice-president of the local Chertsey branch of the Red Cross, which established a rest station at Weybridge railway station under the charge of Dr. Eric Gardner. Voluntary Aid Detachments (known as V.A.D.s) were established by Ethel Locke King, and Auxiliary Military Hospitals were opened in 1914 at various locations. There were eventually 15 hospitals under her care. Brooklands hospital was established in 1915 in Brooklands House and in 1918 it catered for 606 patients. Caenshill, which opened in 1914

129 Injured servicemen outside St George's Hill Military Hospital, *c*.1915. The two men seated in the car are Messrs. Grey and Wood and the man standing just behind the bonnet with his left arm in a splint is Mr. Lester. The nurse was Mrs. E. Kirk, a close friend of Dorothy Grenside who was assistant curator at Weybridge Museum.

130 Caenshill House was the property of Ethel Locke King, and was used as military hospital for the duration of the First World War; it treated 272 servicemen.

131 The Weybridge War Memorial which was unveiled on 23 March 1923.

with 32 beds, lasted until 1918, when it admitted 272 patients; Dr. Eric Gardner was the medical officer there. Llandraff hospital opened its doors in 1916 and by 1918 it had 44 beds and had treated a total of 840 patients. St George's Hill golf course clubhouse had 70 beds by 1918. By 1915 there were 15 V.A.D. units with 700 staff.

At the end of the war, Ethel Locke King was made a Dame of the British Empire in recognition of her work in caring for wounded servicemen.

From 1916 onwards, especially after the Battle of the Somme, casualty figures mounted and local newspapers printed long lists of those killed, wounded or missing in action. A Weybridge War Shrine was unveiled in the churchyard of St James's Church on 25 March 1917 by the Rev. R.A. Buller, with the church choir in attendance. The shrine was a wooden plaque which recorded the names of all local men killed. It was similar to other war shrines that had been unveiled in the district, including Russell Road and Cottimore Lane, Walton-on-Thames. It was not until 1923 that Weybridge acquired its permanent war memorial. This was unveiled on 18 March 1923 next to modern-day Temple Market as a lasting tribute to all those men who did not return from the Great War.

Toc H

Toc H was a soldiers' welfare organisation established by First World War army padres, the Rev. P.B. Clayton and Rev. Neville Talbot, in a house in the Belgian town of Poperinghe in December 1915. The house was rented from a Belgian merchant and converted for use as a chapel, library and rest house, where soldiers of all ranks could find a bed, meal and company away from the front line a few miles off at Ypres, Salient. It was called Talbot House, although to the soldiers it was known as Toc H, the morse code equivalent of the official name. The house provided fellowship for soldiers from all branches of the army, who would not have mixed in civilian life. The attic was turned into a chapel, known as the Upper Room, and the establishment was run by Rev. Clayton. Following the end of the war in November 1918, Rev. Clayton, who was known by his schoolboy nickname of 'Tubby' Clayton, was determined to keep alive the spirit of fellowship shared by all at the house in Poperinghe, and in 1921 Toc H Mark 1 was opened at 23 Queen's Gate Gardens, London. In 1922 King George V granted a Royal Charter of Incorporation to a Toc H of no fewer than 40 branches. At a special ceremony at the Guildhall, London, in 1923, the Prince of Wales lit a bronze lamp with a flame that was used to light lamps for all the other branches of Toc H, many of them abroad.

The Rev. H.C. Money spoke at a meeting in the Weybridge Cinema in January 1926 on the subject of 'What is Toc H?'. A Weybridge branch was quickly established and first met in Dedman's restaurant in Baker Street. Thereafter it moved to *The Newcastle Arms* in Church Street, and in 1928 to the Congregational Church lecture hall in Queen's Road. In 1934 the branch moved again to a building in Minorca Road behind the County Cinema. The branch members undertook jobs within the local community: in September 1938, they were putting on sideshows for carnivals and fêtes, as well as hospital visiting and providing refreshments for nightwatchmen on roads and public works. They were also helping Czech refugees

132 Talbot House, Poperinghe, Belgium, *c.*1962. The house was the headquarters of Toc H during the Great War.

by the end of that year. During this time the branch had set up a ladies' section.

By 1952 branch meetings were held in The Hut in Baker Street, behind Bowman's garage. This burned down on 6 October 1952 and a new Hut was officially opened in 1955. A larger premises opened off the High Street in 1962. Declining membership and the age of most of the existing members led to a decision to close the branch in 1984, the last meeting being a farewell party held on 27 June. The longest serving member of the Weybridge branch was Mr. Eric Wheeler, who joined in 1930 and stayed until 1984.

The Second World War

With regard to the civilian experience, many of the characteristics of the First World War were repeated in the Second, although on a much greater scale. The bombing of towns and industries often resulted in large numbers of casualties. Aggressive submarine warfare by the German navy led to severe shortages, and widespread rationing was introduced for all items of clothing, food, petrol and domestic goods. As in the First World War, military industries flourished in the area, particularly at the Vickers aircraft factory at Brooklands, where the famous Wellington bombers were built. The strategically important Hawker Hurricane fighter aircraft, which were to play a vital role in the defeat of the German air armada during the Battle of Britain in the summer of 1940, were also assembled at Brooklands and flown off to various RAF stations.

By the time of the Munich Crisis in 1938 it was obvious to those in local government that another war with Germany was imminent; it was only a matter of time. From 1937-8 preparations were being made to provide shelter and relief against the expected bombing of civilian targets. A meeting of the Walton and Weybridge Urban District Council was held at *Oatlands Park Hotel* on 19 April 1937 to discuss air raid precautions and to present certificates to six volunteers who had already assisted in preparations over the previous six months. Mr. W.H. Harris, Clerk to the Council, was air raid precautions officer for the Weybridge area at that time.

The council had ordered 30,000 gas masks and 13,000 sandbags (at a cost of £10 per hundred) by 1939 and was in the process of planning a civil defence network. It employed 84 civil defence workers and 828 volunteers by the start of the war. Air Raid Posts were also manned by volunteers. The Weybridge Civil Defence Headquarters was located in the council offices in Aberdeen House, and air raid shelters were built by local people in their back gardens,

133 Soldiers from the 79th Battalion, LAA, RA, on anti-gas drill at Kempton Reservoir in August/September 1939. This unit was formed in 1938 as a territorial unit in the Walton-on-Thames and Weybridge area. In 1939 it was attached to the Royal Artillery as an anti-aircraft unit issued with Bofors guns. The battalion was shipped out to the Far East and captured by the Japanese on the island of Timor in 1942. During the next three years many of the men died in captivity in Japanese POW camps.

134 Volunteers from the Weybridge Home Guard clearing up wreckage at the Electric Furnace Company premises in Queen's Road after enemy action, *c.*1944-5.

often using the famous Anderson shelter. The council built large air raid shelters in the area, one of which was in Churchfields recreation ground. At Brooklands, Vickers built shelters for their own workforce and employed their own team of A.R.P. and civil defence workers. An Invasion Committee was formed by the Council to prepare for the defence of the area should the German Army land in force. The Committee included Superintendent Curry of Weybridge Police Station, and involved Surrey County Council, the local Home Guard, Civil Defence Units, A.R.P. Units and the National Fire Service.

Serious bombing of the area started in August 1940. The earliest and by far the worst incident of the whole war occurred on 4 September 1940, when German bombers broke through the air defences and raided the Vickers factory, killing 83 people, seriously injuring 176 and wounding another 243. The Ball Room in Mount Felix, Walton-on-Thames was used as a temporary mortuary. By the end of December 1940, 97 residents had been killed by bombing and over 1,300 houses damaged or destroyed. In 1941 all people aged 18-59 were registered for civil defence work and the local Auxiliary Fire Service was strengthened.

135 Burvale Cemetery, 1940. The Vickers aircraft factory at Brooklands was bombed by German aircraft on 4 September 1940 and those killed in the bombing were buried here.

136 Painting of a K-75 'Flower' class corvette, HMS *Celandine*, by Geoff Shaw, 1980. HMS *Celandine* was commanded by Lieutenant-Commander P.V. Collings, RNVR, and was deployed as a convoy escort in the Atlantic from 1942-5. The painting shows *Celandine* escorting a convoy that has been attacked by German submarines. The huge explosion in the centre of the picture represents an oil tanker that has just been blown up after being torpedoed. The *Celandine* was adopted by Walton and Weybridge Urban District Council after Warship Week in February 1942.

After the allied invasion of Europe on D-Day, 6 June 1944, the Germans launched their V1 flying bombs at London, many of which overshot their target and landed in the area. A total of 19 fell in Walton and Weybridge. On the night of 16 June 1944 flying bombs landed in Hanger Hill. Before 29 August 18 flying bombs had landed in the locality, killing six people and injuring 26, compared with a total of 119 killed in air raids up until late 1944. Over 2,000 houses were damaged by the V1 attacks in the summer of 1944.

A report compiled by the Walton and Weybridge Council on air raids in the district up until late 1944 found that there had been 829 alerts and 53 air raids, in which 359 high explosive, and 21 oil bombs had fallen, along with 4,800 incendiaries.

In common with the First World War, various campaigns were launched by the government to encourage local residents to give donations towards the war effort. In February 1942 Walton and Weybridge U.D.C. staged a 'Warship Week' campaign, in common with the rest of the country, to raise funds for the Royal Navy. HMS *Celandine*, a 'Flower' class corvette built in 1940, was adopted by the Council after

£500,000 was raised in the Walton and Weybridge area. She saw much action in the North Atlantic on convoy duties and helped sink a U-556 off Cape Farewell, Iceland, on 27 June 1941. She was eventually scrapped in Ireland in 1948. During 1943 the Council staged a 'Wings for Victory Week' campaign which raised £564,000 for the RAF, and helped purchase Wellington bombers. These were built at Brooklands.

Although people knew the war would soon end, everyone was surprised when peace was suddenly declared in May 1945. No one had made any preparations to celebrate the end of the war, and the local authority did not have the resources to organise celebrations. However, people arranged their own street parties bringing whatever could be bought using the ration books. Most of the parties were attended by children, women, and old men, as all the younger men were still away in the forces. The Council did floodlight some public buildings in the area, including churches, but the official peace celebrations were not held until June 1946, when a large military parade took place in the city of London, to which the local authority sent their own representatives.

Bibliography

Barker, J.L and D.M., *A Window on Walton* (1994).

Barker, J.L and D.M., *A Window on Weybridge* (1993).

Barton, Morag E., *A History of Hamm Court Farm* (1972).

The Berkeley Group Ltd., *The Old House, Weybridge* (1982).

Blackman, Michael E., *St George's Hill* (1988).

Blackman, Michael E., *Oatlands and The Golden Ball* (1986).

Bradley, E.N., *A Short History of Weybridge Hospital* (1976).

Brayley, E.W., *A Topographical History of Surrey* (1841).

Browning, Robert, *St George's Hill Golf Club* (*c.*1970).

Cooke, Alan, *Oatlands Palace Excavations 1968.*

Dimmock, S.C., *Weybridge Railway Station 1834-1970.*

Domesday Book—*Surrey* (Phillimore, 1975).

Elmbridge Museum Service, *Brooklands* (1985).

Elmbridge Museum Service, *Camera Studies* (1982).

Gardner, Eric, MB.Cantab, *A Short History of Oatlands 1505-1909* (*c.*1911).

Gardner, Eric, MB.Cantab, *The British Stronghold of St George's Hill* (1911).

Goodhall, M.H., *Flying Start* (1995).

Greenwood, G.B., *A Dictionary of Local History* (1983).

Greenwood, G.B., *Seventy-Eight Years of Local Government* (1974).

Hadlow, S. and Hiskins, A., *Weybridge Ladies' Amateur Rowing Club* (1986).

Hartley, George, *A History of St George's Hill Golf Club, 1913-1983.*

Hewlett, Henry Gay, *Chronicles of Oatlands* (1862).

Kempster, Helen, *History of St James' Parish Church* (1998).

Lake, Christine, *Up Pontes!* (1997).

Lansdell, Avril, *A History of Weybridge Parish Church* (1987).

Lansdell, H.W., *Keep the Home Fire Burning* (1970).

Lansdell, Avril, *The Portmore Story* (1975).

Lansdell, Avril, *The Wey Navigation* (1975).

Le Fevre, Margaret, *300 Years of Local Schools* (1970).

Le Fevre, M., *St George's College, Weybridge* (1969).

Lewis, G.L., *Weighing up Weybridge 1892-1939* (1985).

Leith Ross, Prudence, *The Story of the Tradescants* (1985).

Lindus Forge, J.W., *Oatlands House* (1972).

Lindus Forge, J.W., *Oatlands Palace* (1970).

Lovelock, E., *Reminiscences of Weybridge* (1969).

Malden, Henry Elliot, M.A., *The Civil War in Surrey, 1642.*

Martin, Shirley, *Houses on the Heath* (1995).

Martin, A.G., *Inns and Taverns* (1974).

Pike, Royston, *The Elmbridge Story* (1977).

Potter, John F., *Iron Working in the Vicinity of Weybridge* (1982).

Poulton, Rob, *Archaeological Investigations on site of Oatlands Palace* (1988).

Pulford, J.S.L., *The Locke Kings of Brooklands, Weybridge* (1996).

Oatlands Park Cricket Club 1867-1967 (1967).

Robinson, A.E., *The Parish Church of St James, Weybridge* (1947).

Smith, Reginald A., *The Weybridge Bucket* (1908).

'St George's Hill, Weybridge', *Surrey Advertiser*, Supplement 27 July 1912.

'St Martin de Porres, Weybridge', Souvenir Brochure, 1964.

Symes, Michael M., *Fairest Scenes* (1988).

Tarbut, J.E., *The Ecclesiastical History of Weybridge* (1897).

Tarplee, Peter, *Guide to the Industrial History of Elmbridge* (1998).

Walton and Weybridge Local History Society, *A Short History of Weybridge* (1991).

Walton and Weybridge Local History Society, *Church of St James's, Weybridge* (1979).

Weybridge Cricket Club, *Weybridge Cricket Club* (1974).

Weybridge Museum, *Background to History* (1972).

Wheeler, Lucy, *Chertsey Abbey* (1905).

White, Neil, *Elmbridge Borough in Old Picture Postcards* (1996).

White, Neil, *Walton-on-Thames and Weybridge* (1997).

Woodget, Dudley, *St George's Hill Lawn Tennis Club* (1988).

Index

Bold numbers refer to the illustration page number